The Unreachable Child

Sam B. Morgan

THE UNREACH

ABLE CHILD

An Introduction to Early Childhood Autism

Memphis State University Press

Library of Congress Cataloging in Publication Data

Morgan, Sam B   1932-
    The unreachable child.

    Includes bibliographical references and index.
    1. Autism. 2. Autistic children. I. Title.
RJ506.A9M67   618.92'8982   80-29538
ISBN 0-87870-202-4
ISBN 0-87870-201-6 (pbk.)

COPYRIGHT ACKNOWLEDGMENTS

The author wishes to thank and acknowledge the following for permission to reprint material:

p. 11 From Kanner, L. *Childhood psychosis: Initial studies and new insights.* Reprinted by permission of V. H. Winston & Sons, 7961 Eastern Ave., Silver Spring, MD 20910.

p. 36 Reproduced from the *Wechsler Intelligence Scale for Children—Revised Manual* by permission. Copyright © 1974 by the Psychological Corporation. All rights reserved.

p. 37 From Kanner, L. *Childhood psychosis: Initital studies and new insights.* Reprinted by permission of V. H. Winston & Sons, 7961 Eastern Ave., Silver Spring, MD 20910.

p. 45 From Tinbergen, N. Ethology and stress diseases. *Science*, 1974, *185*, 20-27. © The Nobel Foundation, 1974. Reprinted by permission.

p. 50 From *DSM-III: Diagnostic and statistical manual of mental disorders* (3rd edition). The American Psychiatric Association, Washington, D.C., 1980. Reprinted by permission.

p. 60 From Kanner, L. *Childhood psychosis: Initital studies and new insights.* Reprinted by permission of V. H. Winston & Sons, 7961 Eastern Ave., Silver Spring, MD 20910.

p. 61 From Durant, W. *The story of philosophy.* New York: Simon & Schuster, 1953. Reprinted by permission.

p. 66 From *A Child called Noah* by Josh Greenfeld. Copyright © 1970, 1971, 1972. Reprinted by permission of Holt, Rhinehart and Winston, Publishers.

p. 68-69 from Kanner, L. *Childhood psychosis: Initial studies and new insights.* Reprinted by permission of V. H. Winston & Sons, 7961 Eastern Ave., Silver Spring, MD 20910.

p. 69 From "The Child is fallen." Reprinted by permission from *TIME, The Weekly Newsmagazine;* copyright Time, Inc. 1960.

Acknowledgments

I wish to express my deep appreciation to the people who helped me through the various stages of writing this book and preparing it for publication. Two of my former associates at the University of Tennessee Child Development Center, Marion Birge and William M. Wilson, kindly reviewed the manuscript and offered astute suggestions which helped me to improve the book in both style and content. Dr. Marvin Gottlieb, Editor of the *Journal of Developmental and Behavioral Pediatrics*, also reviewed the manuscript with a keen eye and suggested revisions which resulted in a more readable, informative book.

I extend thanks to Bruce Cohen and W. Edward Amos for their help in checking references and proofing the manuscript, and to June Haire, Felita Gouldin, and Julie Taylor for their contributions in the preparation of the manuscript.

I must also express my gratitude to Alicia Horton, whose sensitive, constructive editing of the final manuscript reflected her appreciation of childhood autism and what I wanted to say about it in this book. I would be remiss, too, if I failed acknowledge my special indebtedness to the autistic children and parents with whom I had contact over fifteen years or so. Their influence on my thinking should be evident throughout the book.

My work on this book was spread over several years, with the bulk being done in fitful spurts on nights, weekends, and vacations. During this period my wife, Pat, and four daughters, Cindy, Melinda, Lisa, and Suzy, showed remarkable patience and good humor in tolerating my preoccupied stares and lapses in social interaction. Although they respected and supported my wish to complete the project, it is nice to know that they would not have thought less of me had I not finished it.

Contents

The Unreachable Child

Introduction

Timmy, a five-year old with large dark eyes in a fragile face, looks like a normal child when you first see him in the waiting room. But after you observe his behavior for several minutes, you sense that something is wrong. He avoids looking directly at you, and when you speak to him, he doesn't respond. All at once he starts spinning gracefully on his toes and fluttering his hands, oblivious to you and the others around him. He stops abruptly and begins to speak in a hollow, sing-song voice. What he says, though, doesn't make any sense. In a high staccato, he recites sequences of the alphabet, as if they have hidden meaning. Then you catch some fleeting phrases, barely audible, "It's going to be a long season . . . Timmy is a good boy. . . ."

He goes to the toy box, takes out a wooden jigsaw puzzle, and assembles it with deftness and speed. You note, though, that he assembles it over and over face down. Through all of this repetitive activity, he has a deliberate, pensive air as if he were trying to order a confused, inward world with outward ritual. You offer him your hand and ask several times, "Timmy, will you come with me?" At first he responds to your hand as some bothersome, inanimate intrusion, brushing it away as if it were attached to a string from the ceiling rather than to a person. He finally grasps it and whispers, "Timmy, will you come with me?"

Timmy shows the symptoms of early childhood autism, a very

3

severe disorder that has baffled and frustrated parents and professionals for a number of years—a disorder with no known cause and no known cure. Of all the behavioral handicaps of childhood, autism is the most bewildering. Autistic children like Timmy have been described from time to time in writings that go back two hundred years. But it was only in 1943 that Leo Kanner (1) defined autism as a special psychiatric syndrome.

Kanner (2) gave the name *early infantile autism* to the bizarre set of symptoms shared by eleven young children whom he had been studying for several years. He chose the word "autism," derived from the Greek word meaning self, to denote the self-contained, or "autistic" existence of these children. He used the term "early infantile" because the disturbance seemed to exist from early infancy on. Since Kanner's original article, however, there have been reports of children who do not clearly reveal signs of autism during early infancy but later show all the symptoms (3). For this reason, the term *early childhood autism* has evolved and is considered by some researchers to be more accurate than Kanner's term. The shortened terms "autism" or "autistic child," however, often are used by professionals in referring to the condition or to the child showing it.

Early childhood autism is somewhat rare, although not as rare as it once was thought to be. Since researchers differ to some degree in defining the disorder, the estimates of incidence vary. If a strict diagnostic definition is used, such as Kanner's, only about one child in ten thousand may meet the criteria for autism (4); in a broadened definition, such as that used by the National Society for Autistic Children, as many as five children in ten thousand may be called autistic (5, 6). For reasons still unknown, autism afflicts three to four times as many boys as girls, with first-born males being especially vulnerable (6, 7, 8).

Since Kanner defined it as a unique disorder in 1943, autism has stirred an interest and controversy greatly out of proportion to its relatively rare occurrence in the population. Autistic children have been the subject of widespread study and vociferous debate in professional and scientific circles. In fact, a scientific journal, the *Journal of Autism and Childhood Schizophrenia,* was founded in 1971 primarily for the purpose of publishing articles and research on autism. In 1979 the name of this publication was changed to the *Journal of Autism and*

Developmental Disorders. In recent years the autistic child has caught the public eye through articles in the press and popular magazines, television documentaries and dramas, and books written by parents, such as Josh Greenfeld's *A Child Called Noah* (9) and *A Place for Noah* (10), and Barry Kaufman's *Son-rise* (11). Why all this interest in this rare disorder? There are several reasons that may account for it.

First, there is an aura of mystery surrounding the autistic child that naturally captivates your attention. There are paradoxes in his appearance and behavior that pique your curiosity and challenge your understanding. He is typically an attractive, well-formed child whose contemplative expression and quick movements give the impression of intelligence. Yet he will not look at you, answer your questions, or respond to you as a person. You want to try to reach him, and you feel, of course, that you are the special person who will penetrate the shell and strike the resonant chord.

Second, the autistic child attracts attention because he presents urgent and striking problems in behavior management for parents and teachers. His detached, disruptive, inexplicable behavior is so much more demanding than that of the normal child that it usually consumes the concentration and energy of his parents. They are constantly frustrated in trying to reach him and control him. When they enroll him in a nursery school or kindergarten, they usually receive, after a day or two, an apologetic call from the teacher, who suggests that some other program be considered since she cannot handle him or draw him into group activities.

Then the parents turn, if they have not done so already, to a professional for help. Too often their experiences with professionals only aggravate their feelings of guilt and futility, especially when they find the cause and responsibility for autism dumped in their laps. In response to this lack of understanding and resources, the National Society for Autistic Children (NSAC) was founded in 1965 and now has local chapters throughout the country. This organization, composed mainly of parents, has brought autism to the public's attention and has aggressively pursued educational and treatment programs designed specifically for autistic children.

A third reason for this great interest, a reason that transcends the fascinating and disturbing behavior of the autistic child, relates to the profound influence that autism has on thinking about factors that determine the development of human behavior patterns, both normal and abnormal. Since autism represents the prototype for "psychotic" behavior, it has been a central issue in fervent debates on the perennial nurture versus nature controversy among behavioral scientists. On one side are those who contend that autism is primarily an "emotional" problem precipitated by the psychological environment, especially the attitude of the mother toward the child. The autistic behavior signifies a withdrawal from a world perceived by the child as hostile and rejecting. On the other side are those who argue that autism is basically an organic disorder that is relatively independent of social factors. The autistic behavior denotes an inability to understand and cope with the world. This controversy has stimulated a great deal of research on autism—research that already has begun to yield some preliminary answers to the questions of what autism is and how it is caused.

An exhaustive review of this voluminous clinical and experimental research is far beyond the scope of this book; such a review would fill several volumes and present a formidable challenge to even the most diligent student of autism. Rather, I have intended to give the reader a general introduction to the intriguing subject of the autistic child and the controversial issues surrounding him—issues that concern definition and diagnosis, treatment and prognosis, and, especially, causation.

The book, I hope, will appeal to several types of readers. The first includes students and professionals concerned with developmental disabilities and childhood behavior disorders. The book may serve as an introduction to autism for some or a means of continuing education on the topic for others. In either case, it is intended to sensitize the reader to complex issues and facilitate a better understanding of not only autism but other childhood disorders and disabilities. I hope that the reader, whether a psychology student, a special education teacher, a speech pathologist, or a pediatrician, will gain some ideas that will lead to further study and research and to more knowledgeable, compassionate work with developmentally disabled children and their parents.

The second group of readers includes parents and relatives of autistic individuals, or other persons whose personal lives have been touched in some way by autism. However, it should be understood that this is not a "how to" book; those persons looking for specific suggestions or guidelines on child-rearing techniques or treatment methods should turn elsewhere. Nonetheless, I feel that the information presented will help parents and relatives of autistic individuals to gain more insight into the disorder and will aid them in realistic decision making and planning. Most important, I think that a better understanding of autism will lighten the burden of guilt and criticism carried by many parents through dispelling misconceptions that they and their relatives and friends may have about the disorder and its cause.

The third type of reader to whom this book is directed is the inquisitive lay person who wants to stay abreast of interesting topics and current issues in the study of human behavior. As mentioned above, autistic children have tremendous appeal not only to professionals and behavioral scientists but to most intelligent persons who may have read about them, seen them on TV programs, or heard about them through conversations. I have tried to make the material more palatable to the general reader by avoiding or translating jargon and specialized terminology in describing the autistic child and discussing the issues. This was not done out of any spirit of condescension but rather as a means of testing the substance of certain ideas and achieving clarity in expression; in the process I discovered that many impressive terms and phrases used in the professional literature serve more to obscure than to clarify. I think that the reader will find that this demystification of language in no way diminishes the mystery of the autistic child.

Part I focuses on the autistic child's symptoms and considers how these compare and contrast with those of other childhood disorders. Part II describes the controversy that has centered on the relative importance of psychogenic versus biogenic influences; this section reviews parental characteristics, major theories of causation, supporting evidence for these theories, and new insights based on recent research. Part III examines the various treatment techniques used with autistic children and summarizes research on the adjustment of autistic individuals when they reach adolescence and adulthood. The final pages reflect on some of the lessons learned and new perspectives gained through study of the short but controversial history of this rare disorder.

The material is presented in a sequence that, in a sense, recapitulates the evolution of scientific thinking regarding the autistic child, proceeding through various stages from the "what" to the "why," from meticulous clinical description to sometimes misleading speculation about cause to insights and explanations based on careful research and long-range study. I make no claim to an unbiased, impersonal coverage of the topic of autism, for I have no doubt been affected by my own experience with these children and with parents whose guilt and confusion have been aggravated by professionals with ready answers based more on theory than fact. Some of the descriptions of autistic children in Part I come from my own experiences with them or from observations of parents. In the course of looking at the autistic child, I think that we will realize that substantial answers do not come easy when we are dealing with the complex, variable, and paradoxical phenomena that constitute human behavior.

1 The Child and His Behavior

Introduction

In 1799 a five-year-old boy was admitted to Bethlehem Asylum in England. The bewildering behavior of this boy so struck John Haslam, the apothecary to the hospital, that he described it in his textbook *Observations on Madness and Melancholy,* published in 1809.

The boy, according to Haslam, never entered into play with other children or showed any personal attachment to any of them. Instead, he played in a preoccupied, solitary manner with toy soldiers for long periods of time, whistling with precision several tunes that he knew. While he knew the names of many things and used expressions that normally convey emotion, he never applied these terms in any personal way. He never referred to himself directly in the first person as "I" or "me" but instead used the third person, referring to himself by name or as "he" (12).

The history of science is full of coincidences and discoveries whose relationships are not immediately apparent. The study of autism is no exception. In the same year that Haslam encountered the boy in England, another boy was captured in the woods of Aveyron, France. Naked and scarred from life in the wilderness, he was estimated to be eleven or twelve years of age. His phantomlike existence had been reported by the people of Aveyron, who had caught fleeting glimpses of him running through the woods searching for food in the form of nuts, roots, and acorns. Until 1799, however, he managed to elude capture. Victor, as the boy came to be known, was taken to Paris where he was put on display like an animal in a zoo and visited by throngs of people. One of the visitors was Jean Marc Gaspard Itard, a young physician employed by the National Institute of the Deaf and Dumb in Paris. Itard viewed Victor as a special challenge and persuaded the authorities to turn the boy over to him for treatment. Itard spent the next five years in trying, with only limited success, to habilitate and educate this strange youngster who had apparently spent most of his life outside the company of other human beings.

In two papers later to be translated and published as *The Wild Boy of Aveyron* (13), Itard described with exquisite sensitivity the unusual behavioral features of Victor. He showed little interaction with people, never looking at their faces but grasping their hands like objects to lead them to whatever he wanted. He resisted even the slightest change in his environment, remembering the exact position of things in his room and vigilantly maintaining their precise arrangement from day to day. His response to sound was quite selective; he showed no response to a pistol fired right behind his head but looked up expectantly when someone quietly cracked a walnut in his vicinity (14).

The significance of the similar behavior patterns of these two boys of drastically dissimilar backgrounds might still be unnoticed had it not been for a series of astute clinical observations made almost 150 years later. In October of 1938, the five-year-old son of a lawyer in a small town in Mississippi was brought to Leo Kanner, director of the Child Psychiatry Clinic at Johns Hopkins Hospital in Baltimore. The boy, whose background and behavior was meticulously recorded by Kanner, was oblivious to people and, although demonstrating an amazing store of verbal knowledge, was unable to carry on a normal conversation. From the time he was two and a half years of age, he could recite accurately the Twenty-third Psalm, the names of all presidents and vice-presidents, and the alphabet both forwards and backwards; he could precisely hum or sing many tunes. He showed a fascination with blocks and pans, spinning them deftly and preferring them to people. He showed an infallible memory in reproducing exact arrangements of objects and was upset with minute changes in environmental stimuli and daily routine. He rarely addressed anyone, but when he did, he referred to himself as "you" and to the person addressed as "I" (1, 15).

By 1943, Kanner had seen eleven children in whose behavior he had discerned certain common features. He published that year his now classic article "Autistic Disturbances of Affective Contact," in which he first described these children, proposing that their symptoms constituted a rare behavior disorder (1). The next year he labeled the disorder *early infantile autism* (2).

Kanner outlined five major symptoms as composing the syndrome of early infantile autism (1, 16). The first and most pervasive was the children's *"inability to relate themselves* in the ordinary way to people and to situations from the beginnning of life" (1, p. 242). The second he described as *"an anxiously obsessive desire for the maintenance of sameness . . ."* (1, p. 245). The third characteristic was the failure of these children to use language for the purpose of communication. The fourth was their fascination for objects and their ability to handle them with dexterity. The fifth was the "good cognitive potentialities" of these children as inferred from the extraordinary skills they demonstrated in certain isolated areas. Although Kanner felt that all of these five symptoms were present in autism, he did not give them all equal significance. He considered the first two to be primary and the other three to be secondary.

When he made his initial observations and defined the syndrome of autism, Kanner was probably unaware of Haslam's and Itard's case histories, but the unusual behavior that he saw in the eleven children bore some uncanny similarities to that seen in the two boys described by the earlier writers. Some researchers, then, have applied the retrospective diagnosis of autism to the boy who appeared at Bethlehem Asylum and to the wild boy of Aveyron (14). Since Kanner's original delineation of the syndrome of autism, innumerable case studies have appeared in the literature but none surpass, or even equal in most instances, the lucid, detailed, engrossing depictions found in the 1943 article. Most professionals concerned with autism still concur with Kanner's contention that it is a distinct behavioral syndrome. Most also accept the major symptoms delineated by Kanner although some may arrange and label the symptoms differently from Kanner and disagree with the priority he gave to certain symptoms (3, 6, 17).

The definition proposed by the National Society for Autistic Children (6), for example, encompasses a wider range of symptoms than those specified by Kanner. According to this definition, the autistic child shows disturbances in: (a) developmental rates and sequences; (b) responses to sensory stimuli; (c) speech, language-cognition, and nonverbal communication; and (d) capacity to appropriately relate to people, events, and objects. These symptoms typically are manifested prior to thirty months of age. With this broader definition, more children will be designated as autistic than will be if Kanner's diagnostic criteria are strictly followed. Although the discussion of autistic symptoms in Part I is organized primarily around Kanner's outline, these symptoms will be related to those noted in the National Society for Autistic Children's definition.

Chapter 1 considers what Kanner felt to be the most basic disturbance in autism—an inability to relate to people in an ordinary fashion or "autistic aloneness." Chapter 2 looks at the autistic child's apparent drive to maintain sameness in his life, which Kanner considered to be the second most important symptom. Chapter 3 presents the baffling disturbances and deficits in the speech and language of the autistic child. Chapter 4 describes the paradoxical and sometimes astonishing intellectual skills of the autistic child. Finally, Chapter 5 examines the problem of diagnosis and how the autistic child is differentiated from children with other developmental and emotional problems.

While it is impossible to separate fully the two questions, Part I deals more with the "what" than "why" of autism. The first reports found in the literature, such as Haslam's, Itard's, and Kanner's, were essentially descriptive, tinged with the wonder evoked by the inscrutable behavior of these children. I hope that the following chapters convey to the reader this same sense of wonder.

1 Autistic Aloneness

When Timmy was about four or five months of age I noticed that he didn't respond to us in the same way as our other children had done. He showed no reaction as I approached his crib. He didn't seem to care whether we were around or whether we picked him up. When I picked him up and held him, he was like a sack of flour at first. Later when I held him, he would hit his head over and over against my shoulder. He also would bang his head in his crib. At this point, we became concerned. As we look back now, Timmy was always unresponsive to human contact, both in a physical and social sense. He always preferred being alone and doing his own thing— over and over.

The symptoms of autism usually appear early in the autistic child's life although the parents may acknowledge them or realize their significance only in retrospect. In most cases the parents, when questioned carefully, can trace the onset of the autistic symptoms back to early infancy; in some cases, parents may report apparently normal development up to eighteen to twenty-four months of age before the symptoms appear (18). It is quite rare for the symptoms to emerge after thirty months of age (3).

Despite the strong likelihood that autism is present in most cases in early infancy, parents may overlook or even deny the subtle signs in their child. While an especially astute, experienced mother may

13

sense that something is wrong when her child is less than six months of age, some parents may wait until the child is six or seven before they acknowledge that he has a significant problem and seek help. Most autistic children, however, are first evaluated at two to three years of age mainly because the parents become concerned over delay in development of speech at that time (3, 8).

Development of First Signs

For the first few months the typical autistic child may be viewed by his parents as healthy and attractive, even precocious and alert (7). At around four or five months of age, however, he begins to show some suggestive signs that, to the trained eye, may distinguish him from the normal infant. The normal infant at this age reacts socially through subtle physical responses that are often taken for granted. When you start to pick him up, for example, he makes an anticipatory adjustment by shrugging his shoulders. When you hold him, he molds his body to fit your posture—that is, he cuddles. These responses are usually absent at this age in the typical autistic child. The mother, especially if she has handled other babies, is vaguely disturbed to find that he shows no anticipatory movements before being picked up and that he goes limp or stiffens rather than snuggles when held in her arms (1, 7, 19), or he may react more aggressively to being held by banging his head against her shoulders, as if he were recoiling from her body.

Since these manifestations that occur during the first year are somewhat elusive, even to the experienced eye, they may be overlooked or minimized by parents at the time. They often describe the autistic infant as a "very good baby" who never frets and rarely cries; in some cases, however, they may report the baby to be extremely irritable and highly reactive to minor stimulation. He appears in most cases, though, to have no need for companionship or social stimulation (8). This lack of positive response to people is revealed through other disturbing physical and behavioral symptoms that may appear during the first or second year. The parents may note that the child prefers rocking in his crib to being held, or they may find him bouncing his head against the mattress, ignoring the presence of anyone near his bed (7).

The mother may also sense some problems during feeding or nursing, especially if she has fed normal infants. The normal baby experiences his first and most basic relationship with another human being during the process of feeding. This relationship serves as the prototype for the development of his social responsiveness to others. He learns that the warm closeness of his mother goes with the pleasant sensation of warm milk in his mouth and belly. Through this gratifying experience he begins to view the presence of human beings in a positive way. For the autistic baby and his mother, however, feeding is not the intimate and mutually satisfying occasion that it is for most mothers and infants. In addition to the absence of cuddling during feeding, he may have problems in sucking, which, of course, interfere with food intake and hunger reduction (20).

When he is introduced to solid food during the second six months of life, the autistic infant frequently shows an abnormal response, as if he were rejecting this intrusion from the external world. The strained foods which are readily accepted by the normal baby are often refused, especially those with rough texture, such as chopped meats (8). He may later spurn certain other foods and develop odd and fastidious food habits and preferences that will last throughout his life (7, 21, 22).

Lack of Visual and Auditory Response to People

We noticed, too, as Timmy got older—about two or so—that he didn't look at us in the eyes. In fact, he seemed to actively avoid looking directly at us. He didn't seem to hear us either. We were beginning to think that he had a hearing problem. But he did respond to sounds, especially music. He would often have a knowing smile on his face, or a frown, but we didn't know why.

For most of us the eyes play an important role in our day-to-day communication with one another. Poets and novelists have expressed this notion for centuries. Du Bartas spoke of the eyes as "windows of the soul" and Cervantes called them "silent tongues of love." Most of us have read or heard at one time or another Ben Johnson's plea for the visual toast. Less poetically, we talk of "eye-to-eye" agreements and describe our most direct human confrontations as being "eyeball to eyeball." We all probably agree that visual interaction reinforces social interaction and is a natural part of our most personal communication with others. Through eye contact, we visually acknowledge each other as "persons."

Before he reaches six months of age, the normal baby shows a positive visual responsiveness to the people in his world. When his mother moves around the room, he follows her with his eyes. When she plays "peek-a-boo," covering her eyes and then abruptly exposing them, he laughs and responds with a twinkle in his eyes. When his mother clucks or speaks softly to him, he coos and gurgles, attending to her face with his eyes.

The autistic baby rarely shows this direct visual interaction with people in his environment (1, 23, 24). Parents report that he appears to respond visually to them as he would to environmental fixtures. Parents recall that their attempts to play "peek-a-boo" or "pat-a-cake" with their ten-month-old autistic baby were a waste of time; teaching him at twelve months to responsively wave "bye-bye" was equally futile. Further, the autistic baby usually reacts to the sight of a stranger in the same indifferent way he reacts to his parents, failing to show the stranger anxiety that most infants exhibit at around eight months of age (8). Nor does he learn to smile as a social response to people whether they are strangers or his own parents.

When he reaches three or four years of age, this failure to look directly at a person's face or eyes is a conspicuous feature of the autistic child's behavior. The terms *avoidance of eye contact* or *gaze aversion* are often applied to this symptom (23). Such terms suggest that the autistic child, like an extremely bashful child or painfully shy adult, shuns eye contact because it is unpleasant or threatening to him. This may be the case, but then it may not be. As discussed in a later chapter, the autistic child may instead be incapable of perceiving or comprehending eye contact as anything special. Eyes may be no more socially significant to him than fingers. Regardless of the cause, his failure to fixate on the face and eyes of another person represents a barrier to social interaction.

This aloneness is also shown in his lack of auditory response to people. Most parents suspect that the young autistic child is deaf since he gives no response when they call his name or speak to him. His ability, however, to repeat accurately things he has heard, such as sayings or musical pieces, precludes a hearing problem. He is capable of receiving sounds but appears to be selective in responding and attending to them (6, 7, 25, 26, 27). While he may show no response to his mother's voice or a baby rattle, he may be acutely distressed by certain incidental sounds, such as the hum of a vacuum cleaner or the distant ring of a telephone. In response to these sounds the young autistic child often cups his hands over his ears with a frown as if he were experiencing sharp earaches (28).

Sounds that normally elicit a direct response to other people are ignored by him or reacted to in parrotlike fashion. When you ask him his name, he may not respond at all or he may echo your question. On the other hand, he may sit entranced for hours listening to music and later hum precisely portions of what he has heard (29). So the autistic child is not deaf, although at times he appears to be. Rather he seems to be engrossed in his own activity, and he shuts out intruding sounds, especially those requiring social interaction.

Preference for Objects to People

Even when he was only one, he began to manipulate objects in a repetitive way. We gave him a set of blocks which he became very attached to. It was rather disturbing to us as parents to see that he cared more for the blocks than for us. His first word, rather than "mama" or "dada," was "block."

The autistic child's social isolation is further revealed in his preference for objects to people. He seems, in fact, to form close relationships with certain objects, relationships that he maintains and guards as we would our most valued and intimate friendships (1, 30, 31). This fascination with objects, which is considered in detail in the next chapter, appears at an early age. Upon entering a reception room or office, the autistic child immediately goes to blocks, toys, and other objects and ignores the people present. He may spend hour after hour arranging objects in a certain pattern or balancing or spinning them. Often the preoccupation is with round objects which he handles with exquisite finesse (7). The child may become quite upset if the objects are taken away or if their arrangement is slightly disturbed. He appears to be content in his world of inanimate objects, so long as there are no incursions by people.

In his examination of children suspected of autism, Kanner has used the "pin prick" test to aid in determining if they respond more to objects than to people. The normal child, when stuck with a pin, usually reacts to the person holding the pin; the autistic child typically responds to the pin and ignores the person (1).

Failure to Communicate with Speech

The autistic child's language, or lack of it, represents another barrier to effective communication with people. Only about one-half of autistic children use speech; the rest are mute or reportedly have spoken only once or twice in their lives (7). Language is rarely used for the purpose of communication by the autistic child who does speak. Up to six or seven years of age, he usually does not respond directly to questions, and he refers to himself in the third or second person rather than the first person (1, 32, 33). His speech is mechanical and idiosyncratic, more related to his own private world than to the human world around him. This bizarre and baffling use of language is discussed more thoroughly in Chapter 3.

Failure to Develop Feelings for Others

From early infancy on, the most disturbing feature of the autistic child is his failure to develop feelings for and relationships with the people in his life, including those who take care of him daily and have the most intimate contact with him (6). The mother of one of Kanner's first cases summed it up quite well by saying, "I can't reach my baby" (1). Although the autistic youngster encounters more and more people as he moves through his childhood years, he never seems to appreciate them in any personal sense. He does not show the cooperative play that is a landmark of social development for normal children between two and four years of age; nor does he develop the friendships which play a vital role in the socialization of most young children (6). He is the quintessential loner.

While he experiences more and more social situations as he grows older, he still remains isolated from the feelings and values of others, showing little social sensitivity and propriety. Seven-year-old Mike, for example, nonchalantly took off his clothes in public, to his mother's embarrassment, or obliviously strolled through groups of playing children. Eisenberg and Kanner (18) reported the case of a four-year-old boy who on a crowded beach walked straight toward his goal even if this entailed stepping on the newspapers, hands, feet, and torsos of surprised sunbathers. He did not deliberately go out of his way to walk on the people, but neither did he try to avoid them.

This lack of awareness of the feelings of others persists in adolescence and adulthood, even in those few autistic persons who make some social adjustment. Eisenberg and Kanner (18) noted this lack of social perceptiveness in one of their more successful patients. The young man, when called upon to speak at a football rally for his junior college, startled the group by asserting that he thought the team would probably lose. His prediction, although valid, was heresy to the assembly who responded with boos. While he was dismayed by their booing, the young man was "totally unable to comprehend why the truth should be unwelcome" (p. 559).

Autistic aloneness is the most inclusive and characteristic symptom of the autistic child. As indicated in this chapter, it is shown in a variety of ways from early in life. The natural tendency is to view this social isolation as a reaction by the child to some social trauma or perceived rejection by people. As plausible and intriguing as this notion may be, other explanations may be just as valid.

Regardless of its cause, the social isolation is nonetheless the most striking and pervasive feature of the child's behavior. It is as if he is insulated by an invisible sheath that blocks the exchange of warmth and affection with other people. The social stimuli that we send him through our touch, our eyes, our voices, never seem to reach him in any personal sense. In fact, he appears to guard against such stimuli, reacting to them as intrusions on his private, self-contained existence—an existence in which he resists change and insists on order and sameness.

2 Security in Sameness

Robert has always been concerned with order and ritual. When he was only two, he would arrange blocks in lines for hours. If we altered this arrangement in even the slightest way, he would become upset. Or if we interrupted his activity, he might fall down, kick, and scream. Now he goes through certain rituals. He strikes the kitchen table and then taps his fingers on it—at least twice a day. He will not go to bed at night until the telephone directory is on the table by his bed and turned to a certain page. Then he gets up several times to check the page before going to sleep.

The changes, both big and small, that are inevitable in our lives present constant problems to the autistic child. He fears the most minute alterations in his world and uses rigorous defenses to guard against them. He is finely tuned to nuances of order in the environment that most of us would ignore or take for granted. If his order is upset, he becomes upset.

Kanner (1) referred to this characteristic in autistic children as an "anxiously obsessive desire for maintenance of sameness" (p. 245). He regarded this feature and autistic aloneness as the fundamental symptoms of infantile autism under which the other symptoms might be subsumed. Like autistic aloneness, this apparent need for preservation of sameness pervades the autistic child's existence and is expressed in diverse ways.

Extreme Sensitivity to Environmental Order and Change

Parents report that the autistic child shows this obsessive concern for order and sameness at an early age. When he is not yet twelve months of age, the autistic baby may respond abnormally to changes in environmental stimulation (8). At times he may become distressed or fearful over sounds that he ignores on other occasions, over changes in room illumination, the feel of certain fabrics, or variations in body position. As he moves into early childhood, he becomes more and more vigilant in keeping the same conditions in his surroundings from day to day. Changes that may be trivial to other children may cause pronounced emotional reactions in the form of extreme panic, violent rage, disconsolate weeping, or tenacious refusal to do something (7). Thomas, when I evaluated him at six years of age, refused to go to sleep at night unless the bedroom door was ajar at a certain precise angle; Robert insisted on wearing the same pajamas night after night. One three-year-old boy described by Kanner (1) was even disturbed when the sun set and when the moon failed to appear in the sky at night.

The acute anxiety that the autistic child experiences with change in the environmental surroundings is illustrated in the case of the autistic boy whose family was in the process of moving to a new home (1). When he saw the moving men roll up the rug in his room, he became frantic. He continued to be intensely upset until the moment he saw his furniture arranged in his new home in the same fashion as before. His anxiety suddenly disappeared, and he walked around fondly patting each piece.

Resistance to Changes in Food, Dress, and Bedtime Routine

The distaste for change often reveals itself in the eating habits of autistic children. Almost all have rigid food preferences, which may differ markedly from child to child. What one autistic child prefers exclusively, the other may spurn. One child accepted no food but milk for the first six years of her life (22); others reject milk altogether (7). One boy would drink only from a transparent container (7); another refused to drink anything from such a container (34). Some autistic children will not drink liquids unless they are at certain precise temperatures. They may be just as unyielding and fussy in their acceptance of solid food. One girl, from the time she was three, would eat nothing but sandwiches she made herself (7). Another child relished chocolate but would only eat it in squares; chocolate in any other form was unacceptable (21).

This resistance to change is also shown in habits of dress (7). Many autistic children want to wear the same set of clothes every day and become quite distressed when they have to change. Others become distraught when their clothes are soiled slightly. Robert, one of my own cases mentioned earlier, threw a fit if one drop of urine got on his underwear.

Bedtime is an occasion that often elicits much more concern in the autistic child than in the normal child (7). The normal four-or five-year-old engages in some routine or ritual (and a great deal of procrastination) in preparing for bed each night. He may kiss his parents, recite a prayer, ask to be tucked in with a favorite doll or teddy bear, and then, after his parents have settled back into their easy chairs, request the inevitable drink of water. The autistic child at this age may demand less conventional and more elaborate routines and arrangements. He may insist every night on the same pajamas and bedclothes, the same arrangement on his dresser, the same window opened to the same height, and so forth.

Ordering of Objects

This persistent and often frenetic need for arrangement is displayed vividly in the autistic child's behavior with objects. When presented with an unstructured group of objects, he usually tries to impose some arbitrary order on them. Once he has done so, he also regroups the objects in the same pattern on subsequent occasions, showing infallible memory in reproducing the original arrangement (1, 33). Four-year-old Jeff, for example, whom I observed, revealed this tendency over and over while taking an intelligence test. On one part of the test he was asked, after a demonstration by the examiner, to string beads of three different shapes—square, round, and cylindrical. The shapes were irrelevant to the test; in order to pass, Jeff needed only to string four beads in two minutes. Instead of stringing the beads as the normal four-year-old would do, he immediately aligned the beads in three neat rows according to shape. When the examiner picked up one of the beads out of a row, Jeff grunted in protest, snatching the bead from the examiner's hand and restoring it to its position. When presented with the beads several days later, he quickly reconstructed his original pattern.

Stereotypic and Ritualistic Motor Behavior

In his apparent attempts to keep sameness in his world, the autistic child fearfully avoids new activity and engages in ritualistic, repetitious actions for long periods of time. In fact, much of his bizarre, eye-catching appearance can be attributed to his peculiar mannerisms and motor behavior, referred to by Ornitz and Ritvo (3) as disturbances of motility. These stereotypic or seemingly programmed movements, though also common in severely retarded individuals (35), are so characteristic of the autistic child that some writers now refer to them as "autisms" (36).

The autistic child often shows this stereotypic motor behavior during infancy. He may rock in his crib for hours or repeatedly bang his head against the mattress or side of the crib (7). As he grows older, he may daintily toe-walk around the house, spin his body like a top, or dart and lunge in staccato fashion (3, 37). These movements do not have the constant, persistent quality of those in the "hyperactive" child but rather are intermittent, usually interrupted by periods of immobility and posturing (3).

The most typical stereotypic actions of the autistic child involve the hands and arms (38, 39). In such actions, he usually moves his hands within his visual field and then studies his hand and finger movements much as a normal six-month-old baby does when he first discovers the intricacies of his hands (3). He often shows unusual posturing with his hands and arms, holding his hands at peculiar angles and weaving his fingers together while regarding them out of the corner of his eye. At certain intervals, he may flap or oscillate his hands and arms, or rhythmically snap his fingers as if he were tuned to some internal metronome. He persists in these activities even in the presence of other persons or toys that would be distracting to the normal child (40). It is interesting to note that the flapping and oscillation of the hands have been shown to occur at the same rate over time in a given child and that groups of autistic children tend to flap at the same rate (39, 41). Ornitz and Ritvo (3) reported that when they examine an autistic child, they have him look at a spinning top. This often evokes motility disturbances such as hand-flapping, posturing, and twirling.

Inexplicably, the autistic child sometimes adheres to this repetitious motor behavior to the point of self-mutilation (42). This self-injurious behavior most frequently takes the form of head-banging, gouging, and scratching (43). The head-banging in infancy is often a harbinger of later head-banging that is injurious (8). It is not uncommon for the autistic child with such tendencies to beat his head against a wall until blood is drawn and brain damage threatened. The treatment for this perplexing self-destructive behavior is discussed in a subsequent chapter.

Fascination and Facility with Objects

When Danny was about two, he became attached to certain objects which he had to have every day. He would balance books on the end of a table and would bang his head if they didn't balance. He became especially fascinated with jar lids of various sizes and still spends a great deal of time arranging and spinning them. He's real good at jigsaw puzzles and can put them together very quickly. In fact, he can put them together much faster than either my husband or I. We've noticed, though, that he always leaves one part out of every puzzle. If we put the part in, he will immediately remove it.

Much of the autistic child's quest for sameness centers on inanimate objects. He shows a relentless preoccupation with certain objects which he manipulates in fetishlike fashion. In handling these objects he often demonstrates consummate skill. This fascination and facility with objects is one of the diagnostic features of autism (1). As previously mentioned, the autistic child prefers objects to people. He displays a fondness for those objects that provide him pleasure and meet his needs, and anger toward those that defy his manipulation, such as a piece that will not fit into a puzzle.

The toys that absorb the normal child's attention are shunned by the autistic child or reacted to inappropriately. The dolls and toy cars that a normal three- or four-year-old plays with in a purposeful manner are ignored or manipulated or arranged in some idiosyncratic fashion (8) The autistic child usually focuses his attention on other things that fit his penchant for repetition. He shows a fancy for mechanical gadgets such as light switches, tape recorders, and faucets (7). He may spend hours turning a light switch or faucet on and off. Five-year-old Mark would punctually drop by his principal's office en route to class each morning to ritualistically push in and pull out the different control buttons on the video-tape recorder and TV set stored there. With a contented smile, he continued his routine until pulled from the room. Throughout it all, he never acknowledged the presence of the principal.

Many autistic children are mysteriously drawn to round objects, which they can handle deftly. Reports have been made, for example, of three-year-old autistic boys who could balance dimes on edge (21, 44). Another boy, obsessed with balls, could catch a ball with either hand at fourteen months of age (7). Danny, when he was only two, had a collection of jar lids which he balanced and twirled with amazing dexterity. This fascination with spinning of circular objects, such as jar lids, is common among autistic children.

The autistic child's enchantment with circularity or roundness is difficult to explain. Perhaps the symmetry, wholeness, and redundancy of a circle or circular activity have a special appeal to the child's need for order and sameness. It is common for autistic children to whirl their own bodies or sit for hours entranced with the spinning turntable of a phonograph. Danny, who showed the exquisite touch in twirling jar lids, demanded Cheerios for breakfast every morning. He would then take the Cheerios and make circles around his plate. He also spent a great deal of time forming circles with his hands, intently staring at them with a pensive expression.

The autistic child, then, makes his world as changeless, as predictable, as repetitious, as redundant as he can. The new places, new dishes, new clothes, new activities, and new friends that enrich our lives as we move through childhood and adulthood are to him frustrating, intolerable impositions. We wonder whether his compulsive behavior is an active defense against a world that he perceives as full of rejecting and hostile people, or perhaps it is merely his way of "making sense" of a welter of stimuli that he is not equipped to cope with.

Whatever the reason may be, he resists new stimuli fiercely, responds inflexibly to them, and tries to impose an arbitrary, egocentric order on them. If he talks, this order is revealed in his idiosyncratic, rigid, repetitive use of language—a topic so baffling and complex that it warrants treatment in a separate chapter.

3 Echoes and Metaphors

David was sitting by his mother in the corner of the waiting room. As I got closer, I could hear him reciting in a soft monotone. "Hubert Humphrey died . . . Hubert Humphrey died." Then he smiled to himself. I said, "Come with me, David," and he said in a whisper, "Come with me, David," and took my hand without looking at me. As we left his mother in the waiting room he said, "I left my heart in San Francisco."

Much of the mystique surrounding the autistic child derives from his baffling use of language. Some people have gone so far as to assign to his utterances a sphinxlike quality, full of profound wisdom if the riddles could be unravelled. While it is doubtful that the autistic child's speech has mystical significance, it does present an intriguing problem whose solution may be central to an understanding of childhood autism.

The language problems of the autistic child are more understandable if, first, a distinction is drawn between the terms "speech" and "language." In his book on the language of autistic children, Churchill (45) pointed out that both humans and parrots speak, but only humans have language. Speech refers to the specific ability to articulate sounds that can be recognized as words; language refers to the broader and higher ability to communicate through meaningful expression and comprehension of the spoken or written word or gestures. Many deaf

27

mutes, for example, who lack the ability to speak, may communicate and comprehend concepts effectively through sign language or gestures; conversely, many myna birds may learn to speak but none can communicate or comprehend. Some researchers, such as Rutter (46) and Churchill (45), think that the speech of autistic children may or may not be impaired, but their language is inevitably impaired, usually to a severe degree.

From the start, Kanner (1) was concerned with the autistic child's language deficit, which he called a failure to use language for the purpose of communication. However, he thought that this problem was secondary to the basic problems of autistic aloneness and preservation of sameness. As noted in a later chapter which discusses theories of causation, some researchers (45, 46, 47) now think that the language impairment is the basic problem in autism with the other features being secondary.

Recent research has indicated that indeed most autistic children, including those who speak, show significant retardation in language development (48, 49). In fact, the most frequent complaint of parents is a delay in speech development when the child is about two years of age (3). Many autistic children, then, are initially seen at speech and hearing clinics for speech delay or suspected hearing loss before the diagnosis of autism is considered. These early deficits tend to persist, since autistic children generally perform on language tasks far below the level expected for their chronological age. The typical six-year-old autistic child, for example, functions at the three-year-old level or lower on most language tests. Further, his scores on these language tests are well below his mental age on certain nonverbal tests (49, 50, 51).

Even though all autistic children probably share some degree of language impairment, the speech and language abilities vary a great deal from child to child (49). As noted before, only about one-half use speech; most of the others are either totally mute or they reportedly developed early speech during the first year or so and then lost it soon afterward (7, 8). A few have been known to speak only once or twice in a lifetime in emergency situations. For example, one five-year-old boy described by Kanner (16) had never been heard to utter one articulate word until he became frantic when a prune skin stuck to his palate. He cried distinctly, "Take it out of there!" and then resumed his muteness. There is also the taciturn case of Jonny (44), who had said only two phrases by the age of ten: "I can't!" and "Go to hell!"

In those autistic children who do develop speech a wide range of individual differences exists in the ability to communicate with others, that is, to meaningfully express and comprehend ideas. One child may be limited to single words whereas another less impaired child may be able to use meaningful sentences in dialogue (52). Early speech and precocious vocabularies are often reported in many autistic children who do talk (7). At first the parents may marvel over some of the linguistic feats of their child, thinking that they surely have a prodigy on their hands. As previously mentioned, the first autistic child seen by Kanner (1) could, at only two years of age, flawlessly recite the Twenty-third Psalm, the names of all presidents and vice-presidents, and the alphabet forwards and backwards. After a while, however, the parents' amazement and pride turn to puzzlement and concern. They begin to notice that the child's speech, while precocious in some respects, appears to have little social meaning. The child appears to be speaking more to himself than to other people.

The speech of most autistic children is hollow, parrotlike, and sing-song with no spontaneous inflection, failing to convey any subtle emotion (53). Some speak in barely audible tones, and whispering is common (7). Their words, however, are usually clearly articulated and easily understood in echoed expressions but not necessarily in spontaneous speech, which is typically limited (52). Their speech often is more related to objects than to people, as in the case of Danny whose first word was "block" rather than "Mama" or "Dada" or "Bye-bye." They frequently name objects but rarely answer questions. Strangely, the words "I" and "yes" are almost always absent from their speech until the sixth or seventh year of age (1, 7).

When the speaking autistic child reaches four or five, his peculiarities of speech become more conspicuous and draw more attention. Kanner (1,32,33) was the first to provide a detailed description and analysis of these peculiarities, and most of his observations have been verified in subsequent research. Two of the most typical features reported by Kanner and later investigators are *echolalia* and *reversal of pronouns* (e.g., 7, 8, 59).

Immediate and Delayed Echolalia

Perhaps the most consistently found feature of the speaking autistic child's language is echolalia—the precise repeating of words, phrases, sentences, and questions that he has heard. This repetition may be immediate or delayed. One common form of immediate echolalia in the autistic child is called *affirmation by repetition* (1). Most normal children when asked if they want to do something reply with a "yes" or "uh-huh" or nod of the head. The autistic child typically affirms the question by repeating it; thus, when you ask him, "Do you want to go?" he replies affirmatively by saying, "Do you want to go?" This affirmation by repetition is illustrated by Michael, who during the course of a psychological evaluation began to squirm and show signs of having to go to the bathroom. When asked, "Do you want to use the bathroom?" he quickly replied, while impatiently unzipping his trousers, "Do you want to use the bathroom?"

The autistic child's speech is also characterized by *delayed echolalia* (1). This occurs when a child repeats in a seemingly irrelevant situation a phrase that he has heard at one time or another. The phrase may be a proverb or saying, TV commercial, song title, or a sentence spoken by someone he has had contact with. David, for example, would say in cryptic fashion from time to time, "I left my heart in San Francisco." Tim would repeat the phrase, "It's going to be a long season." Parents report that the child gives no sign of hearing these phrases when they are originally used by someone else. The child may appear to be completely oblivious to the speech around him, such as a TV commercial or a parental comment, and then later repeat to astonished parents the phrase with identical words and inflection.

Many of these "delayed echoes," though peculiar or apparently irrelevant in ordinary conversation, have definite meaning when their origins are traced. Kanner (30) pointed out that these seemingly nonsensical utterances are in many cases *metaphorical expressions* which have a definite referent for the child.

We are all familiar with the metaphor as used by the poet and novelist and even by ourselves in our more inspired moments of speech. According to the *American Heritage Dictionary* (55) a metaphor is a "figure of speech in which a term or phrase is transferred from the object it ordinarily designates to an object it may designate only by implicit comparison or analogy, as in the phrase *evening of life*" (p.

825). Despite the obvious difficulty that lexicographers have in comprehensibly defining them, metaphors (with the possible exception of mixed ones) usually aid and enrich our spoken and written communication. With the autistic child, however, the metaphorical expressions have no communication value or meaning to others unless the specific personal experiences from which they are derived can be established. These expressions have a very private significance to the child.

Kanner (32) has provided a number of fascinating illustrations of the use of metaphorical language by autistic children. Five-year-old Paul, for example, was heard to say at the clinic, "Don't throw the dog off the balcony." Since there was no dog or balcony around, the remark appeared to be irrelevant. Kanner learned, however, that three years previously Paul had been reprimanded by his mother for throwing a toy dog off the balcony of a London hotel. She had used the words, "Don't throw the dog off the balcony." Since that time, Paul used that exact phrase to scold and check himself when he was about to do something that he felt he should not do.

As an infant, Elaine had a collection of toy animals of which she was quite fond. Whenever she cried, her mother told her that the toy dog or rabbit did not cry. So she learned to say, when trying to hold back tears, "Rabbits don't cry" or "Dogs don't cry." By the time she was seven she had a variety of other animals; and when upset, she walked around repeating the seemingly nonsensical words: "Seals don't cry." "Dinosaurs don't cry." "Crayfishes don't cry."

The autistic child uses these metaphorical expressions in an arbitrary way. To paraphrase Humpty Dumpty, when the autistic child uses a word, it means just what he chooses it to mean—neither more nor less. He has his own private, individualized semantic system whose code cannot be broken by a dictionary or thesaurus but only by either direct observation or recall of the incident or stimulus with which an expression is associated.

This point is illustrated clearly by Kanner's case of Donald (32). When he was five years old, he was observed to be scribbling with crayons while earnestly saying, "Annette and Cecile make purple." The key to this baffling statement was discovered when it was learned that he previously had named five bottles of paint after the Dionne quintuplets. Blue became "Annette" and red, "Cecile;" hence, when

"Annette" and "Cecile" were mixed, they became purple. Since purple was not one of the five original colors, it was still referred to as "purple."

This metaphorical language may also involve numbers, as exemplified by two more of Kanner's cases (1). Five-year-old Anthony had puzzled Kanner by frequently expressing his fondness for "fifty-five." Kanner discovered the key to this riddle when Anthony happened to speak one day of his two grandmothers, saying, "One is sixty-four, and one is fifty-five. I like fifty-five best." Knowing that one grandmother had reared Anthony with great patience and affection while the other had shown little interest in him, Kanner recognized that Anthony's seemingly nonsensical preoccupation with this number was really his private way of expressing affection for his grandmother. This idiosyncratic use of numbers is further illustrated by Kanner's first case Donald, who was asked, as part of a test, how much money would he get back if he bought four cents worth of candy and gave the storekeeper ten cents. A person with no knowledge of geometry would have missed the meaning of his cryptic reply, which instead of "six cents" was "I'll draw a hexagon."

Reversal of Pronouns

Another puzzling feature of the autistic child's language is his reversal of pronouns (1). He usually repeats personal pronouns exactly as he hears them. For example, if he once is told by his mother, "I will give you some candy," he may ask for candy on future occasions by saying, "I will give you some candy." Thus, he refers to himself as "you" and to the person addressed as "I." He repeats not only the words, but the inflection. If the mother's remark was in the form of a question, the child's reproduction has the grammatical form and inflection of a question. The child may also refer to himself in the third person. Instead of saying, "I want to go outside," he says, "Jimmy wants to go outside."

As with the metaphorical expressions, the autistic child's reversal of pronouns and referral to himself in the second or third person may be confusing to the naive observer. The case of Jimmy, who is discussed in more detail in the next chapter, serves as a good example. When I saw him at four years of age for an evaluation, Jimmy was extremely precocious in composing words and sentences with a SCRABBLE set, spending a large portion of each day in this activity. Though he never spoke in direct response to questions during the evaluation, he at times responded with *SCRABBLE* tiles to questions composed with *SCRABBLE* tiles. After Jimmy had spent an hour or so composing various words and phrases, I used the tiles to spell out, "DO YOU WANT TO GO?" Jimmy responded by spelling with the blocks, "YOU ARE OK." I accepted this as a compliment and did not realize until later, when reviewing the video-tape of the session, that actually Jimmy was referring to himself in the second person.

This reversal of pronouns usually persists in the autistic child until about six or seven years of age, at which time he gradually learns to refer to himself in the first person and to the person being addressed in the second person. During the transitional period he may occasionally revert to the earlier form, referring to himself in the second or third person (7). The autistic child's tendency to reverse pronouns has been a pivotal point in the classic controversy over the nature of autism. Does his failure to use first person pronouns represent an active negation of his selfhood and an anxiety about speaking of himself to an alien outside world? Or does it reflect a general inability to comprehend, or attach meaning to, concepts, including the concept of selfhood in himself and others?

Literalness and Part-Whole Confusion

The autistic child sometimes shows two other anomalies in language that are mentioned here briefly—*extreme literalness* and *part-whole confusion* (1, 11). Extreme literalness applies when the child inflexibly attaches words or phrases in a concrete or literal manner to specific things or activities. Kanner (1) provided examples of this in his original article. Donald's father wanted to reward him for saying "yes" by carrying him on his shoulders. Donald did learn to say "yes" but only as a request to be carried on his father's shoulders. The word "yes" was used exclusively in its original literal sense. Further, when Donald was requested to put something "down," he put it "down" in a literal sense, that is, always on the floor. John would correct his father's references to pictures "on the wall" by saying they were "near the wall" (which literally they were).

Part-whole confusion is illustrated in the case of the three-year-old autistic boy who asked for dinner by saying, "Do you want some catsup, Honey?" His favorite dish was meat seasoned with catsup. He used this phrase, which pertains only to part of a meal, as a reference to a whole meal (7).

Later Language Development

If the autistic child fails to use language consistently for communication by five years of age, then he probably will never develop advanced speech. Further, he will show no appreciable intellectual development as he approaches adolescence and will appear more and more retarded, especially if the bizarre motor activity diminishes (8). On the other hand, if he develops communicative speech by his fifth birthday, he usually will continue to use it in a very literal manner as he grows older, showing limited ability to apply it in any abstract way. His speech, while communicating concrete ideas, is devoid of emotional tone and is inflexible. In turn, he has difficulty in comprehending the subtle social and emotional concomitants of speech in others (47).

The various features of the autistic child's language reviewed in this chapter appear on the surface to be quite puzzling and complex. Perhaps, though, his language has been made more complicated and mysterious than it really is by our reading too much into it. Perhaps we have projected our own symbols, preconceptions, and theories into words and phrases that he may be using in a literal, rote, uncomprehending way. Most of the language peculiarities observed in the autistic child appear to have a common element: They involve the automatic, precise reproduction of the language that the child has heard and has associated with specific events. A phrase learned in connection with a specific event may then be generalized to similar events; that is, the phrase may be automatically elicited by stimuli similar to the original event.

The autistic child's language system is, in many respects, like that of a tape recorder. He selectively records, stores, and plays back the language input from his environment with no changes in person or inflection. He hears himself referred to by others in the second or third person and therefore refers to himself in the same way. He hears the question, "Do you want some candy?" with the presentation of candy and thereafter reproduces the phrase when he wants more. David's phrase, "I left my heart in San Francisco," however plaintive its ring, does not refer to some ego-shattering event he experienced in that city. He just happened to register the song title in association with some specific situation; and when he encounters that situation or similar ones, he replays it.

A later chapter emphasizes the crucial role that language plays in whether or not the autistic child makes some adjustment to society as he grows older. This critical function that language serves in determining the severity and prognosis in autism has led some researchers to the conclusion that the autistic child suffers basically from a language disorder (45, 47, 56). Others think that he has a broader cognitive disorder or a special form of mental retardation (7). The next chapter presents the ways that he differs from the typical retarded child.

4 Islets of Brightness

In the introduction to his widely used intelligence test for children, David Wechsler defined intelligence as "the overall capacity of an individual to understand and cope with the world around him" (57, p. 5). If we accept this somewhat general definition of intelligence, then we have to conclude that most autistic children are indeed intellectually retarded since they appear to be deficient in understanding and coping with the world. Most of these children, especially the younger ones, are inaccessible for standardized intelligence testing, and the IQs that can be obtained on them usually fall well within the mentally retarded range (6, 58). Also like the retarded child, they are deficient in adaptive or coping skills. Yet the autistic child differs significantly from the typical retarded child. When you look carefully at him, you catch glimpses of isolated areas of ability that are sometimes astounding, but often misleading.

Physical Appearance and Early Development

Todd is a healthy-appearing three-year-old with beautiful blond features. As he flits around the playroom, he anxiously seeks out objects that he can spin. The most striking thing about his appearance is his facial expression. Such a serious, intent expression appears to be quite incongruous for a boy who is barely three. He abruptly stops his activity and holds his right hand at a peculiar angle, making a circle with his thumb and forefinger. For several moments he studies the circle with a perplexed frown, as if he were pondering some abstruse philosophical problem.

Although he may be markedly impaired in dealing with the world, the autistic child does not have the physical appearance of the severely retarded child. Rather than presenting a vacuous facial expression, he usually has a preoccupied, pensive air, as if he were rapt in deep thought (7). In his original article, Kanner noted the "strikingly intelligent physiognomies" of autistic children, describing their faces as giving the "impression of *serious-mindedness* and, in the presence of others, an anxious tenseness" (1, p. 247).

They are also attractive children with well-formed physiques and appealing, often delicate, facial features. Lorna Wing (59) attributes part of the physical attractiveness of many autistic children to an element of immaturity in their appearance and to the unusual symmetry in their faces. Autistic children, like normal children, show variations in size, with some being small for their age and others being of average or above-average size. Regardless of their size, though, they give the impression of being younger than they really are and convey a "kind of vulnerable innocence" that evokes protective responses in people who have contact with them (59).

Most autistic children have none of the physical stigmata or congenital anomalies associated with certain forms of mental retardation and which facilitate an early diagnosis. Nor do these children typically show the significant neurological impairment that frequently accompanies retardation of a moderate to severe degree (60). Although some may be clumsy or poorly coordinated, many are graceful and agile in movement with a consummate touch in fine motor skills (7, 59).

In further contrast to the typical retarded child, the early developmental milestones of many autistic children are not consistently delayed although disruptions in rates and sequences of development may occur (61, 62). Many may show motor development that is on schedule or even advanced; like the normal infant, they sit with minimal support at about six months of age and walk around one year. Others, however, may show erratic motor development with spurts at one time and lags at another (3).

This inconsistent development of abilities also applies to speech and language skills. As mentioned in the last chapter, those autistic children who talk will often develop early speech (7). Some, however, may start talking early and then mysteriously stop; and some may show an initial delay before they start (3). The classically autistic child may learn words at an astonishing rate during the first two years and utter, to the surprise of his parents, a complete sentence before using the component words singly. One child, for example, learned between his seventh and twelfth months the following sequence: "mama," "dada," "bear," "spoon," "hungry," "done," "ball," and "C'mon, let's play ball" (7). In addition to surpassing the retarded child in early acquisition of words, many autistic children show speech that is more clearly articulated and more grammatically complex than that of retarded children (49, 63). In fact, the early speech of some autistic children is more clear and complex, although certainly less functional, than that of normal children of the same age.

Special Motor and Visual-Spatial Skills

Chapter 2 noted some of the extraordinary feats in fine motor coordination and manual dexterity that distinguish many autistic children from mentally retarded children. Autistic children often perform well on nonverbal tasks requiring visual-spatial and manipulative skills, such as putting together jigsaw puzzles, dismantling and assembling mechanical devices, and building constructional toys (6, 59). At early ages, many can complete with dazzling speed the Seguin Form Board test, which requires them to place eight different geometric forms into appropriate slots (7, 64). On the Wechsler Intelligence Scale for Children (57) they generally do relatively well on the Object Assembly test and the Block Design test, both of which are timed tests involving construction of objects and designs (65). While the performance of some autistic children is well above age level on these visual-motor tasks, it should be noted that the average or even below average performances of many autistic children tends to stand out in contrast to their extremely low scores on most other tasks, especially those requiring verbal and symbolic abilities (59). Although these isolated peaks of visual-motor skills distinguish the autistic child from the retarded child, the autistic child applies them in rote fashion; he may, for example, assemble a jigsaw puzzle just as fast with the picture down as up (7).

Some autistic youngsters are good at drawing, although the drawing may be rigidly done. When I saw eleven-year-old David, he could draw a picture of a person in exquisite detail. Each feature, however, consisted of a geometric form—the head a perfect circle, the eyes circles filled with concentric circles, the nose a triangle, and so forth. His picture looked, in short, like a mechanical man, a composite of stark angles and curves, devoid of humanness. When scored according to age norms, however, it yielded an IQ above average. Another autistic child, evaluated several years later, produced an eerily similar geometric man, which he could reproduce with unerring accuracy even after a lapse of several days. When he was presented with a sheet of paper and told to draw a man, it was as if a button had been pressed on an automaton, activating an electronically preprogrammed set of motions that produced the drawing like a computer printout.

Rote Memory Skills

Another skill that is typically well-developed in autistic children is rote memory (6, 59). The speaking autistic child often has an abundant, though idiosyncratic, store of language that indicates a capability for rote learning and a sometimes amazing memory for verbal items. He appears to record and store items in his memory for long periods of time precisely as they were originally experienced. The items chosen for storage do not appear to have any special significance to normal people, and they are stored verbatim with no interpretation or changes (59). Some children remember TV commercials, poems, songs, sayings, conversations they have overheard, and bus and train routes. If they read, they may spend hours memorizing and reciting details from television schedules or advertisements from the yellow pages.

One eleven-year-old boy whom I saw had an almost inexhaustible repertoire of proverbs that he forced into different situations. The use of a given proverb appeared to be triggered by sound association. For example, when asked, "Why does oil float on water?", he quickly replied, "Oil's well that ends well." When asked to define the word "recede," he answered, "If first you don't recede, try, try again."

These special skills shown by autistic children may also involve memory and manipulation of numbers (59). Some can do long numerical calculations in their heads, and some have been known to have inexplicable calendar abilities, giving the correct day of the week for any date in the last hundred years. Although they may remember numbers, they may not always be able to apply them appropriately. For example, one autistic girl was able to write out the multiplication tables from two to twelve but was unable to answer such questions as "What is three times four?"

Even if the autistic child is mute and therefore incapable of demonstrating verbal memory through speech, he usually reveals a precise memory for nonverbal things. As mentioned in Chapter 2, he remembers exact arrangements of objects in the environment and becomes upset when he detects a nuance of change. He often displays a remarkable facility for regrouping such items as blocks or beads in the same pattern after a lapse of several days (7, 33). If a part is missing from the original complement, he may grunt, scream, or flutter his hands frantically until it is restored to its place.

Special Reading Skills

When he comes into my office, David goes immediately to the telephone directory and begins to rhythmically read advertisements in the yellow pages. The words come out in a soft, mincing lilt, each syllable distinct. "Our chrome-plated crankshafts are magnafluxed—heat treated and ground to specifications." He flips the pages, his eyes barely glancing at each page. "Study cosmetology. The South's most advanced beauty school. Government approved courses."

Some autistic children reveal precocious skills in reading and spelling. It is not uncommon to find autistic children who are reading by the time they are three or four years of age or even before they talk (7, 66). One astonished mother reported that she had no notion that her young child could read until he read the words on the back of a cereal box while walking with her down the aisle of the grocery store. Another stated that her child first displayed his precocious reading ability by reading billboards while riding in the car.

Some young autistic children are preoccupied with reading aloud such material as advertisements and entries in the telephone directory. For example, two autistic boys whom I saw, both six years of age and strangers to each other, showed an uncanny similarity in their reading skill and taste, preferring to read over and over the yellow pages of their local telephone directory. The *TV Guide* is also a favorite of many autistic children who read.

The prodigious reading and spelling ability of some young autistic children is illustrated in the case of Jimmy, whom I saw when he was four years of age. Since it was known in advance that Jimmy spent a great deal of time at home playing with lettered blocks, a *SCRABBLE* game was brought to the testing room. After Jimmy had quickly completed the Seguin Form Board, he was presented with the *SCRABBLE* set. With unerring accuracy and speed, he immediately began composing words with the lettered tiles, softly reading each word as he made it, "ARTHUR FIEDLER WITH THE BOSTON POPS . . . MAGNAVOX. . . ." He stayed absorbed in this activity for almost an hour, putting on an astounding display of verbal skill. He spelled several words beginning with the letter "Q," always following it with "U." He nimbly composed from "Z" to "A" the letters of the alphabet, with the tiles evenly divided into two rows of thirteen each. He also spelled some neologisms (for example, "ZEDOVAK," "LADOVAK") which he enunciated phonetically. Although he would not respond to oral questions with speech, he would at times answer questions through the *SCRABBLE* medium, referring to himself in the second or third person. When he apparently wanted to leave the testing room, he spelled the word "EXIT."

Jimmy's ability to use his reading and spelling skills in meaningful communication is exceptional for an autistic child. In most other autistic children, the skills can be quite misleading. When we see a five-year-old who reads fluently such words as "transmission" and "cosmetology," we are impressed. We soon discover, though, that his reading, like other features of his language, is done rotely with little apparent comprehension (67, 68). There is the visual input and the vocal output with no behavioral indication of intervening understanding.

Cobrinik (66) explained these rote reading skills on the basis of the isolated facility for pattern recognition that many autistic children have. From an early age they often show highly developed visual imagery and visual recall relating to nonverbal patterns, abilities that are also basic to reading. To these children, words may merely represent complex spatial patterns that are instantaneously processed like subway maps.

Specific Musical Talents

A number of cases have been reported of young autistic children who show astounding musical talent, including perfect pitch and the ability to accurately reproduce complex musical pieces. Kanner (1) referred to these skills in his original article, noting unusual musical activities in six of the eleven children described. Sherwin (29) provided a fascinating account of three musically talented autistic children, two of whom are identical twins. One of the twins could at fourteen months reproduce notes of the scale with "extraordinary accuracy of pitch." At seventeen months, he could repeat a complete aria from *Don Giovanni* and before he was three sing "a remarkable repertoire of music, consisting of symphonies by Mozart and Haydn, songs by Schubert and Brahms, selections from *Carmen*, a Tchaikovsky piano concerto, and diversified well-known songs" (p. 825). He refused to sing on request, but would reproduce the melody upon hearing it sung by someone. If the last note of the tune was omitted, he would correctly furnish it. His twin brother, although not quite as accomplished, was absorbed in listening to music from at least eighteen months of age. He was especially interested in folksongs, which he could sing perfectly.

O'Connell (69) reported the strange case of Joseph, an eight-year-old boy with perfect pitch who curiously combined music and geography. In areas other than music, he functioned at a severely retarded level. When given any sound, Joseph could immediately find the key on the piano to match it; he could also play without hesitation the melody and accompanying chords of familiar tunes in any prescribed key. He would not voluntarily go to the piano to play a tune but could be coaxed to do so with the promise of a marshmallow. He would, however, spontaneously play a seemingly meaningless series of notes in much the same fashion that he spoke seemingly nonsensical phrases. O'Connell discovered that Joseph "had actually abstracted the principles of tonality (music written in a key) which are taught to music majors in most college theory courses" (p. 225). The geography came in with the reference to the diminished seventh chords. He showed a peculiar fascination for these chords, which he used to designate the four directions of the compass. Lansing (70) suggested that Joseph had this fetish for the diminished seventh because it resists inversion (that is, sounds the same regardless of which note is put on top) and hence fulfilled his autistic need for sameness.

Although the majority of autistic children do not show such exceptional musical talents as those described above, most reveal a love for music in one way or another. Some listen to music for hours on end, apparently entranced by the repetitious beat of certain pieces. Some of the more talented children learn to play an instrument and, in a few cases, compose music (59). One of Kanner's earliest cases, who represents one of the rare instances of apparent recovery from autism, has become a composer as an adult (7). A very small number have become piano tuners as adults, having the requisite combination of perfect pitch and manual dexterity (59).

The special abilities discussed in this chapter—the motor and spatial skills, verbal and nonverbal memory, early reading skills, and musical talents—appear in different mixtures and degrees in autistic children. One child may show a precise memory for spoken language while another may be mute with finely tuned motor skills. More recent studies have shown that the level of functional intelligence may vary greatly in autistic children (51, 71, 72). About sixty percent of autistic children have IQs below fifty; twenty percent have IQs between fifty and seventy; and only twenty percent have IQs of seventy or higher (6). Further, more and more evidence, which is examined more closely in a later chapter, indicates that two-thirds to three-fourths of all autistic individuals will continue to function throughout life at retarded levels (3, 73). Nevertheless, the autistic child is different from the typical retarded child. While the intellectual profile of the retarded child is fairly even and predictable, the intellectual profile of the autistic child is erratic and paradoxical.

It was these isolated peaks of ability that prompted Kanner originally to use the term "good cognitive potentialities" as a part of the diagnostic description of these children. Many people assumed, then, that the autistic child's poor performance on certain tests was due to refusal to perform rather than inability and that these peaks of ability were representative of the child's "true intelligence." If the emotional problems could be eliminated, then the overall intellectual functioning would rise to the level of the peaks, and the child would be normal.

Hindsight now shows that these assumptions are probably invalid because the "potentialities" are seldom fulfilled as the child grows older. As discussed in a later chapter, these specific skills, however brilliant they may appear at first glance, are rarely coordinated into an adaptive intelligence that allows the autistic person to understand and to cope flexibly with his world. We could speculate, as some have done, that many of these children were genetically inclined toward high intelligence but something went awry along the way and only fragments of giftedness remain. Such a notion becomes more plausible when we look at some of the research on their parents. But first, we should consider some of the diagnostic problems that professionals face when confronted with a child suspected of having autism.

5 Diagnostic Dilemmas

In his acceptance speech for the 1973 Nobel Prize, the ethologist Nikolaas Tinbergen (74) expressed concern over the lack of agreement in the diagnosis and labeling of autistic children. "If the art of diagnosis has any objective basis," he stated, "there should be a positive correlation between first and second opinions" (p. 20). Citing a study by Rimland (75) which demonstrated the absence of such a correlation in the diagnosis of 445 children with severe behavior disorders, Tinbergen observed: "What these doctors have been saying to parents is little more than, 'You are quite right; there is something wrong with your child' " (74, p. 20).

Despite this lack of agreement in diagnosis from doctor to doctor, Tinbergen acknowledged that autism represents a "relatively well-defined cluster of aberrations" if the term is used "in the descriptive sense of Kanner's syndrome" (74, p. 20). The last four chapters have examined this "cluster of aberrations" found in the autistic child—his inability to interact with people, his perpetuation of sameness in his surroundings and behavior, his failure to use language as a communicative tool, and his paradoxical intellectual profile. As strikingly unique as this set of symptoms may appear, diagnostic problems have arisen because the symptoms rarely emerge in clear, well-ordered fashion to form the full-blown syndrome of autism. They may also appear in varying degrees and combinations in children with other disorders

45

and disabilities. These children, though failing to show the full con-
stellation of symptoms, may be erroneously classified as having early
childhood autism on the basis of one or two autistic features. Further,
the terms "autism" and "autistic" have come into such vogue in recent
years and have been bandied so glibly in professional circles that many
clinicians probably are primed to leap to hasty diagnostic conclusions
and to apply the labels too readily (76). But even the most cautious
diagnostician may have problems in some cases in distinguishing the
autistic child from children with other disorders. This chapter discusses
some of the difficulties both clinicians and researchers have in defining
and diagnosing autism; further, it examines some of the childhood
disorders that may show overlapping symptoms with autism—disorders
that create diagnostic dilemmas. Before looking at these disorders,
however, we should first consider some of the problems inherent in
the process of diagnosis of behavior disorders in general and autism
in particular.

Diagnosis of Behavior Disorders

To most people the word *diagnosis* has an omniscient ring to it,
imparting a note of finality to any examination or evaluation. The
literal meaning of the word lends it even more authority. To *diagnose*
means to "see through" an illness, which is literally done in some
cases, as when a tumor is revealed by an X-ray. In other cases the
underlying disease process may be inferred from a set of physical symptoms and then confirmed with laboratory tests, as in diseases of metabolism like cretinism and phenylketonuria (PKU). With most
behavior disorders and deficits, however, the diagnosis is much more
tenuous and tentative. But to anxious, desperate parents groping for
answers and possibly grasping at straws, any diagnostic label may be
something to hang on to. To their ears, it may be the final word, and
it may mean more to them than it actually should.

Diagnosis, as used in most psychiatric or behavior disorders or
impairments, is merely the assignment of a label that serves as a
shorthand term for a set of related behavioral features that may or may
not be associated with demonstrable organic or environmental causes.
If underlying causal factors can be discovered, the diagnosis has more
depth and carries more weight in effective prevention and treatment.
PKU, as discussed in a later chapter, dramatically illustrates this level

of diagnosis. With many behavior disorders or deficits, however, diagnosis is done at a more superficial level, in a literal sense. It consists of weighing and sorting behavioral signs to see if they fit any known cluster of symptoms for which there is an available label. (In the case of autism, Kanner could find no existing label that adequately covered the symptoms of the children he saw, so he coined a new diagnostic term in 1944.) If a child shows a certain set of abnormal symptoms to a sufficient degree, then he may be diagnosed as "mentally retarded" or "schizophrenic" or "aphasic" or "autistic," and so on. In most cases, then, the so-called diagnosis, rather than being an explanation of the behavioral symptoms, is only a description of them.

Problems in Labeling Childhood Disorders

Within the past decade some parents and professionals have become more and more concerned, and even alarmed at times, over the careless use of diagnostic labels for childhood problems. Their concern appears to be at least partially justified. Some professionals attach labels with wild abandon, assigning them indiscriminantly to children whose behavior only partially fulfills the diagnostic criteria of a certain disorder. To complicate matters further, there may be a lack of agreement from one professional to another on the criteria that define the same label. This inconsistency in definitions contributes to the lack of correlation in diagnoses referred to by Tinbergen (74). The child labeled as "autistic" by one doctor may be labeled as "aphasic" by another or "atypical" by another.

Another problem with labeling is that some professionals may give little thought to the effects that the label may have on the child and his life. In some cases the label assigned may be more harmful than helpful to the child and his family. But once a child is stamped, the ink is often indelible. Labels have certain connotations, sometimes erroneous and misleading, for parents, teachers, and other persons who may influence the child. Some labels, unless appropriately qualified and interpreted, may have fatalistic implications and lead to self-fulfilling prophecies. A mildly retarded child labeled only as "retarded" with no further explanation may be branded by teachers as totally incapable of learning and hence given limited opportunity to learn. The next few chapters consider the profound effect that the label "emotionally disturbed" has had on the lives of autistic children and their parents.

In addition to assigning labels cursorily and inconsistently, professionals frequently misinterpret them to parents. Descriptive labels are presented in circular fashion as explanations for the child's behavior. A professional, after a lengthy evaluation of a child, may sit down with the parents and say in a pontifical manner, "Mr. and Mrs. Jones, we feel that Jimmy behaves the way he does because he has early childhood autism." Mr. and Mrs. Jones then ask the logical question, "Doctor, how do you know Jimmy has early childhood autism?" The doctor replies, "Because he behaves the way he does."

There is an old Latin proverb that translated means: "The abuse should not prohibit the use." The tautalogical and unreliable use of diagnostic labels should not preclude their appropriate use. If strict definitions and stringent criteria are adhered to in arriving at a label, that label can be useful in summarizing a set of symptoms even though it may not explain them. Moreover, the question of agreement on precise descriptive criteria for a behavior disorder must be resolved before the variables that cause the disorder can be isolated, whether these variables be psychosocial or organic. In short, the question of "what" must be settled before the question of "why" can be answered. At least some of the controversy concerning the cause of autism, considered in Part II, can be attributed to the lack of agreement regarding the descriptive criteria (77).

Problems in Defining and Diagnosing Autism

Leading scholars in the area of autism, such as Kanner (76) Rimland (7, 75) and Wing (59), have strongly urged that the diagnosis of autism be carefully determined. They think that parents have been misled, treatment misguided, and research issues clouded by indiscriminate use of the term autism and by the lumping of it with other conditions that may show overlapping symptoms.

The lack of consensus in the diagnosis of autism is, of course, related to the diversity in definitions used by diagnosticians. More specifically, clinicians and researchers differ in the criteria they use in deciding whether or not a child is to be diagnosed as autistic. Freeman (77) and Freeman and Ritvo (78) have conducted detailed reviews of the different diagnostic systems and have discussed the confusion involved in the use of them. This inconsistency in diagnostic criteria has contributed a great deal to the conflicting results and conclusions of studies on autism. Some researchers have attempted to alleviate some of the confusion by transforming the descriptions of the syndrome into objective checklists and rating scales of symptoms and behavior. Rimland (7), for example, has developed a detailed diagnostic checklist that has been used extensively in research on autism; Freeman (79) is currently refining an objective system for the diagnosis of autism.

Lengthy behavioral checklists, however, are rarely used by the busy clinician in the diagnosis of autism. In most cases, he probably forms a "clinical impression" based on the degree to which information on a given child (that is, developmental and social history, medical findings, behavioral observations, and psychological test results) measures up to his own set of criteria for autism. The number of children diagnosed as autistic depends upon which set of criteria he has adopted for clinical use.

If Kanner's strict criteria are followed, no more than one child in 10,000 will be labeled as having autism (4); these children are those that are usually referred to as "classically autistic." If the broader criteria of the National Society for Autistic Children (NSAC) are used (6), then as many as five children in 10,000 will be called autistic. As Wing (59) has pointed out, diagnosis is relatively easy with classically autistic children, especially those who show the characteristic speech patterns and islets of ability. Diagnosis is much more difficult, however, in children who show different shades and blends of the disorder. Part of the difficulty, in Wing's view, is related to the fact that many clinicians and researchers have used Kanner's "abstractions" rather than studying firsthand his actual descriptions of the children.

The definition of autism that probably will be the most widely used in clinical practice is that outlined in the third edition of the *Diagnostic and Statistical Manual of Mental Disorders* of the American Psychiatric Association (17). This manual lists autism under the general category of *pervasive developmental disorders*; these disorders, which consist mainly of childhood psychoses, are characterized by marked distortions in the timing, rate, and sequence of many basic psychological functions.

The manual specifies the following six diagnostic criteria for infantile autism:

(a) onset before thirty months of age; (b) pervasive lack of responsiveness to other people (autism); (c) gross deficits in language development; (d) if speech is present, peculiar speech patterns . . .; (e) bizarre responses to various aspects of the environment, e.g., resistance to change, peculiar interest in or attachments to animate or inanimate objects; (f) absence of delusions, hallucinations, loosening of associations, and incoherence as in schizophrenia (pp. 89-90).

These criteria, which relate directly to the features discussed in the first four chapters, include aspects of both Kanner's and the NSAC's definitions.

Even with criteria that are agreed upon by diagnosticians, the diagnosis of autism is complicated by the fact that autism is a developmental disorder, diagnosed early in childhood and characterized by changes in the clinical picture as the child grows older (77). As discussed in a later chapter, the long-term picture in adolescence and adulthood varies greatly in persons who shared the childhood diagnosis of autism. The disorder in one individual may gradually become indistinguishable from schizophrenia; in another, it may slowly assume the form of mental retardation. In order to refine the diagnosis of autism and perhaps define meaningful subgroups, we must, as Freeman pointed out, "understand thoroughly the natural history of the syndrome" (77, p. 143).

With these problems concerning diagnosis in mind, we can now consider some of the childhood disorders that may be confused with autism.

Mental Retardation

One condition that often shows overlapping symptoms with autism is that of mental retardation. The last chapter looked at some of the abilities that distinguish the autistic child from the typical retarded child. Despite these differences, the basically autistic child is often confused with the child that is basically retarded. On the other hand, the child with primary retardation may sometimes be called autistic because he shows one or two autistic features. In many cases, whether to call a child autistic or retarded becomes a somewhat arbitrary decision based on the number of autistic symptoms shown and the presence or absence of clear-cut organic pathology associated with retardation. The diagnostic problem is further confounded by the fact that mental retardation itself is not a physical illness but rather a behavioral deficit—a deficit that may be associated with, or caused by, a diversity of diseases or organic factors. In many retarded children, as in autistic children, no such underlying causes can be clearly determined.

In the United States the most widely used definition of mental retardation is that proposed by the American Association on Mental Deficiency (80). According to this definition, mental retardation refers to "significantly subaverage general intellectual functioning existing concurrently with deficits in adaptive behavior, and manifested during the developmental period" (p. 5). The subaverage intellectual functioning is determined by the child's performance on standardized intelligence tests; the deficits in adaptive behavior are ascertained by a study of the child's early motor development, his learning of social and self-help skills (such as toileting, feeding, and dressing), and his ability to deal with his environment in a practical way.

Many autistic children, in terms of this definition, would be classified as primarily retarded if it were not for the differences that were noted in the last chapter—differences that really may not make a big difference in their adjustment to life. So, a fine line exists between autism and mental retardation, and the two diagnoses are not mutually exclusive. As more and more evidence indicates, the two disorders can clearly coexist, at least in a functional sense (3). Wing (81), for example, interviewed the parents and teachers of all the severely retarded children in one area in London and discovered that about one-fourth of these children had many features of autism, although few could be termed "classically autistic." The autistic behavior, however, could not predicted from the level of intellectual functioning or the IQ score. Many of the children who performed poorly on IQ tests, particularly those with Down Syndrome, were sociable and communicative, showing none of the features of autism; on the other hand, children with relatively high nonverbal abilities but limited communication skills tended to show many autistic features.

It is quite plausible, as a later chapter shows, to regard autism, like mental retardation, as basically a cognitive impairment—an impairment, however, that results in a different set of behaviors than those found in most retarded children. It is also possible that there may be common organic causes underlying autism and certain forms of mental retardation. Nevertheless, to preserve the integrity of the label "autism" the distinction should be maintained between the classically autistic child and the generally retarded child who may show some autistic features.

Perhaps the most common autistic feature seen in children who otherwise are significantly retarded is stereotypic motor behavior (35, 82). As mentioned earlier, some writers refer to these stereotypic acts as "autisms" (36). It is not at all unusual to see severely retarded children engage in ritualistic rocking or even self-abusive behavior such as headbanging or biting. Those autistic children who do show such behavior are those that appear to be the most severely retarded (59). The stereotypic behavior of most autistic children, however, typically involves repetitive motions in front of the eyes whereas that of most retarded children more often involves vestibular and motor stimulation such as rocking (83).

As Wing (59) has noted, other autistic features can be found in severely retarded children. Some may be fearful of change in routine and environmental stimuli, but they usually lack the sensitivity typical of the autistic child. Some may exhibit echolalia, but it is usually the immediate rather than the delayed type associated with autism. Some severely retarded children may even show lack of affective contact but typically not to the degree that the autistic child does. All of these features usually appear in isolated fashion in the retarded child and therefore would not warrant the diagnosis of autism since the full complement of symptoms is not present.

Childhood Schizophrenia

Most experts agree that at least at a descriptive level the diagnostic line between classic autism and mental retardation, although sometimes fine, is real. Some think, however, that the line between autism and childhood schizophrenia is artificial. In psychiatric terminology both autism and schizophrenia are classified as forms of *childhood psychosis,* the generic term for the most severe behavioral disturbances of childhood. Since no underlying disease entity or clear-cut causes have been ascertained, the term childhood psychosis refers to a set of associated behaviors that appear in certain children—behaviors that are severely disordered and interfere markedly with the children's relating to people and coping with the world. Most experts (e.g., 3, 7, 59, 84) categorize autism as a special form of childhood psychosis separate from childhood schizophrenia, but some (e.g., 53, 62, 85) still regard it as an early variant of childhood schizophrenia.

While there are some overlapping characteristics between autism and childhood schizophrenia, there appear to be critical differences that set autism apart as a distinct behavioral entity. Bernard Rimland (7) has constructed a diagnostic check list, used widely in studies with autistic children, to aid in differentiating the autistic child from the schizophrenic child. In his book *Infantile Autism* (7), he has devoted an entire chapter to the discussion of these differences. Other scholars (e.g., 3, 14, 84) have also given considerable attention to specifying the points that distinguish the two disorders.

First of all, there appear to be clear differences in the onset and the developmental course of the two disorders (7, 84). The autistic child typically shows deficits from the start of life or very early in life; the schizophrenic child usually exhibits his aberrant behavior after an initial period of apparently normal development. The autistic child's symptoms follow a steady developmental course; the schizophrenic child's symptoms wax and wane with marked relapses or remissions. The autistic child usually shows good physical development and is in excellent health; the schizophrenic child shows problems in physical development and is generally sickly.

There are differences, too, in the way they respond to people and the world (7). The first chapter noted the lack of physical, auditory, and visual responsiveness to people in the autistic child. As an infant, he does not cuddle; as he grows older, he does not appear to hear people or visually interact with them. The schizophrenic child, in contrast, usually clings and molds as an infant and generally responds directly to people with his eyes and ears as he grows older. While the autistic child stays aloof and detached from his world, the schizophrenic child appears confused and intensely anxious about his world, frequently expressing deep concern about his relationship with it. The autistic child is constantly impervious or unresponsive to people; the schizophrenic child is alternately reaching for and shrinking from people. Further, the hallucinations and delusions characteristic of the schizophrenic child are not experienced by the autistic child.

The symptoms of autism are typically more specific and clear-cut than those of schizophrenia, which are more diffuse and varied (7). Schizophrenic children do not show as saliently the "islets of brightness" described in the last chapter, such as the fine motor facility, rote memory, musical skills, and spatial abilities. The language patterns of the schizophrenic child, while bizarre, do not have the stereotypic "tape-recorder" quality of the autistic child. The language anomalies of affirmation by repetition, pronoun reversal, and delayed echolalia are usually absent in the schizophrenic child.

Finally, there are differences in the family characteristics and sex distribution (7, 84). The parents of classically autistic children are generally more intelligent than those of schizophrenic children and have a lower divorce rate. In addition, the incidence of psychosis or other forms of serious mental illness is much, much lower in the family backgrounds of autistic children. While autism occurs about four times more frequently in males than females, schizophrenia occurs at about an equal rate in both sexes.

Despite these differences that seem to exist between early childhood autism and childhood schizophrenia, some classically autistic preschoolers appear to "grow into" childhood schizophrenia between the ages of eight and twelve years (3, 86); and some autistic children may later show the clinical picture of schizophrenia when they reach adulthood (85, 87, 88). Ornitz and Ritvo (3) described two cases of autistic boys who developed schizophrenic symptoms in middle childhood. One of the boys, who had been clearly diagnosed as having autism at four years of age, presented a schizophrenic picture at age nine. When asked why he rocked, he replied, "The floor is coming up at me" and "the walls are moving in on me." Another nine-year-old, who also had an early history of autism, responded to a question about his hand-flapping by saying, "I am pushing the thoughts back in my mouth." These bizarre verbal responses are more characteristic of schizophrenia than autism.

The following excerpt from a case study of an eleven-year-old child whom I saw illustrates further the diagnostic dilemma that some children present. While showing some characteristics of childhood autism, Billy appeared at this age to be more schizophrenic than autistic.

Billy, an obese boy with large, slanted eyes and a pallid face, was extremely fearful about coming to the testing room. When I asked if he would come with me, he put his head in his mother's lap, pouted like a much younger child, and shook his head in refusal. After his mother and I cajoled him for a short while, he reluctantly agreed to come, saying, "OK, but I'm not going to open my mouth." Once inside the room, he was quite fearful—and labile and inappropriate in emotional behavior. He laughed very loudly in an unpredictable manner, and his mood flitted from sullenness to elation in an instant. His language behavior was extremely bizarre, but yet revealed a precocious vocabulary and memory for sayings. He spoke in a high-pitched, tremulous, sing-song voice, and usually after saying something meaningless, would laugh nervously and quizzically look at me and ask, "Get it?" His first comment upon coming into the room was, "I'm just an old Scrooge." When he sat in the chair, he shrank away from me, narrowed his eyes, and said fearfully, "I'm so scared of everything." Throughout the session he would spontaneously parrot sayings such as, "a bird in the hand is worth two in the bush,"or "too many cooks spoil the broth." He repeatedly made self-disparaging remarks about his performance on the tests and about himself in general. For example, when trying to do a task, he would frequently wring his hands desperately, grab his head, and say with a sob, "I'm just a failure." Throughout the session he showed extreme confusion and poor concentration, for example, "The answer is in my mind all muddled up." His visual-motor coordination was extremely poor on drawing and puzzle tasks.

Symbiotic Psychosis

Another childhood psychosis that shares symptoms with autism and schizophrenia is symbiotic psychosis, an extremely rare disorder first described and labeled by Margaret Mahler (89). Many professionals working with childhood behavior disorders may go through their entire careers without seeing a symbiotic child. Nevertheless, such children exist, and present interesting contrasts and similarities to classically autistic children.

In contrast to the autistic child, the symbiotic child shows the initial psychotic symptoms between two and one-half and five years of age after apparently normal development. Instead of ignoring the mother, as the autistic child does, the symbiotic child is morbidly attached to her, showing intense panic and anxiety when separated even momentarily from her. He clings to her both physically and emotionally as if attached by an invisible umbilical cord. This pathological attachment appears at an age when the normal child is beginning to develop an independent identity and relationships with persons beyond the mother. The symbiotic child fails to develop such an identity apart from the mother and therefore cannot relate as a separate person to others. He shows an extremely low frustration tolerance, becoming intensely panic-stricken over slight changes in routine and minor frustrations. He is hell-bent on doing his own thing; if thwarted, he becomes extremely irritated or agitated, often throwing severe and prolonged temper tantrums over some seemingly trivial frustration. He lacks curiosity, initiative, and aggressiveness, and, as the disorder develops, shows bizarre speech and behavior.

Strangely, the symbiotic child looks more and more like the autistic child as the disorder progresses. He develops secondary symptoms that overlap significantly with those of the classically autistic child. He becomes seclusive, speaks bizarrely, and goes to great lengths to maintain sameness in his environment. In many cases, by the time the child is seen by a professional his behavior may have progressed to a point where it is virtually indistinguishable from autism (90). The two disorders primarily are differentiated, then, on the basis of the early history of the symbiotic child's intimate attachment to the mother (91).

Developmental Aphasia

Another childhood condition sometimes confused with autism is *developmental aphasia* (or *specific language disorder*), which generally is of two types—*expressive* and *receptive*. The child with expressive aphasia shows a specific inability to express or encode his thoughts into coherent spoken language. The child with receptive aphasia exhibits a specific inability to comprehend or decode the speech of others. Some children may manifest a combination of expressive and receptive language problems.

Because of his difficulty in communicating and understanding spoken language, an aphasic child may have some secondary problems in relating to people. He may even show some autistic features, especially if he is under five years of age (59, 92). His frustration in trying to communicate with words may lead to unusual social and emotional behavior. His language deficits, along with the possible behavioral aberrations, may therefore give an initial impression of autism. A close look, though, shows that the aphasic child, unlike the autistic child, communicates in some way or at least tries to do so (71). He interacts socially and attempts to convey his thoughts to others. He may struggle to find the appropriate word to get his ideas across or he may resort to nonverbal gestures and expressions in trying to express himself. If he wants something that he is incapable of asking for, he will point to it or use some other suitable gesture. Furthermore, he responds appropriately to the gestures and expressions of others. The autistic child, in contrast, rarely shows this type of goal-directed communication, or "communicative intent" (93). Nor does he show the appropriate emotional expressions that usually accompany the nonverbal messages of the typical aphasic child.

Some aphasic children may exhibit immediate echolalia, but they usually do not display the delayed echolalia typical of the speaking autistic child (46, 94). Further, aphasic children generally demonstrate comprehension of ideas when they are translated into visual form, whereas autistic children appear to have problems in understanding ideas regardless of the form in which they are presented. In trying to distinguish between autism and aphasia, then, we must observe the child's ability to use nonspoken symbols (59). The child with a pure aphasic disorder should, like a deaf child, learn alternative modes of communication fairly easily. In addition, he can play imaginatively with dolls and other toys, showing an appreciation of their function; the autistic child, in contrast, shows no apparent comprehension of their function and tends to manipulate them stereotypically.

While both the autistic child and the aphasic child reveal language problems, there appear to be certain basic differences in the nature of these problems and the accompanying social and adaptive behavior. In fact, some researchers (e.g., 45, 46) think that the autistic child has by far the more severe and pervasive disturbance of language.

Deafness and Blindness

Like the aphasic child, the child with undetected congenital deafness may show language deficits and a lack of responsiveness that might be confused with autistic symptoms (59). Conversely, the autistic child, because of his failure to respond to certain auditory stimuli, may be initially suspected of being deaf. A hearing test, however, reveals that the autistic child is capable of responding to sound, albeit in a selective fashion. The truly deaf child may develop some social and emotional problems as a result of the sensory deprivation and his frustration in trying to understand and communicate in a soundless world. But, like the aphasic child, he still tries to interact with people in his world. His eyes, rather than ignoring your face and eyes, are actively searching for subtle visual cues and nuances of expression that will aid him in communicating with you.

He demonstrates, too, an understanding of concepts and symbols presented through the visual modality and performs relatively well on general intelligence tests that do not require hearing, such as the Leiter International Performance Scale. In further contrast to the autistic child, he readily learns alternative means of communication such as lipreading or sign language. As Wing (59) pointed out, the deaf child quickly loses his "autism" once he learns to communicate through these other methods.

The child with partial or complete blindness may show self-stimulatory movements and mannerisms that may at first glance resemble the bizarre motor behavior of the autistic child (95). Upon close examination these "blindisms," which may include rocking or gesturing with the arms and hands, are seen to occur in response to environmental stimuli, and they lack the stereotyped, repetitive quality of the hand-flapping characteristic of autistic children. In addition, the blind child typically develops an interest in his surroundings and relatively normal relationships with people (3). Further, his speech and language abilities develop normally or may even be advanced.

While most blind or deaf children are not autistic, children suffering from partial blindness and deafness associated with maternal rubella show a relatively high incidence of autism (96). These findings and their implications are discussed in Part II.

It is beyond the scope of this chapter to cover all of the disorders or conditions that may be erroneously labeled as autism. I have focused on those that present the most frequent diagnostic problems. I should point out, however, that autism may also be confused with elective mutism (97), epileptic seizures (3), anaclitic depression (3, 98), and psychosocial deprivation (3, 59).

Autism, then, may share some common behavioral symptoms (and possibly some common underlying causes) with other childhood conditions such as mental retardation, childhood schizophrenia, language disorders, and sensory impairments. Any given child may show various measures and blends of symptoms that are difficult to sort out. Still, there are children who remain after careful sorting as clearly autistic, manifesting essentially the same set of symptoms meticulously described by Kanner in 1943. The next few chapters discuss the controversy that has surrounded these children, a controversy that begins with their parents.

II The Controversy Over Cause

Introduction

> We must, then, assume that these children have come into the world
> with innate inability to form the usual, biologically provided affective
> contact with people, just as other children come into the world with
> innate physical or intellectual handicaps. If this assumption is correct,
> a further study of our children may help to furnish concrete criteria
> regarding the still diffuse notions about the constitutional components
> of emotional reactivity. For here we seem to have pure-culture examples
> of *inborn autistic disturbances of affective contact.* (1, p. 250)

Kanner's concluding words to his original article on autism set the
stage for a debate that is still unsettled. The debate has centered on
the specific issue of the primary cause of infantile autism, but it has
also served as a forum for the more general issue of the relative importance of environmental or psychogenic factors versus biogenic factors in the causation of behavioral or emotional disturbances. On one
side are people who argue that autism is primarily a socially induced
disorder brought on by the family environment. On the other side are
those who contend that autism is basically the result of an organic
defect (or combination of such defects), and in the middle are those
who maintain that autism is caused by both social and organic factors.

The debate concerns not only the cause of autism but also the
related question of the basic nature of the disorder. Most proponents
of the psychogenic theory view autism as primarily an "emotional" or

"affective" disorder that manifests itself in this bizarre set of symptoms. Most advocates of the biogenic position, on the other hand, consider autism to be basically an intrinsic defect in perceptual-cognitive abilities with the emotional and social problems being secondary signs. Kanner's original theory, as stated in the passage above, did not fit neatly into either of these categories since he proposed that it was an innate affective disturbance.

The controversy over the cause and the nature of this relatively rare disorder relates directly to the speculations of the great philosophers on the basic nature of the mind of man. This controversy has its philosophical roots in classic empiricism on one hand and classic rationalism on the other. The empirical philosophers, exemplified by John Locke, stressed the notion that all knowledge comes through experience. The essence of this philosophy is retained through the catchword *tabula rasa*—the "blank tablet" mind of the newborn upon which experience writes. The child's developing brain, according to this view, is a passive recipient of incoming sensations that become stored as impressions; these impressions in turn are associated in different ways through the child's unique experience. As the radical empiricist William James put it, the newborn infant experiences the raw input as "one great, blooming, buzzing confusion" that is shaped and refined gradually into order and meaning through contact with the outside world.

The rational philosophers, such as Immanuel Kant, argued that the mind or brain of the child, rather than being a passive organ, is an active one with inherent capabilities for imposing structure and meaning on the incoming sensations. As Will Durant (99) so lucidly conveyed Kant's basic thesis, "the mind of man . . . is not passive wax upon which experience and sensation write their absolute and yet whimsical will; . . . it is an active organ which moulds and co-ordinates sensations into ideas, an organ which transforms the chaotic multiplicity of experience into the ordered unity of thought" (p. 202).

So with early childhood autism, the speculative arguments of these philosophers emerge as immediate scientific questions. Does the autistic child behave so strangely because he lacks inherent facilities for organizing or attaching meaning to his world? Or does he behave that way because his experience with his social environment has been different in some way? Is the basic defect in his brain or in the outside world?

These questions regarding the cause and nature of autism are the main concern in Part II as the discussion turns from the "what" to the "why." The answers to these questions will have far-reaching theoretical and practical implications. Autism represents the most profound disturbance in relating to people; and most people, including many professionals dealing with emotional and social problems, naturally assume that such a disturbance in social behavior inevitably must be brought on by social factors. As pointed out in the following chapters, they may be wrong in assuming this about autism.

The discovery of the cause (or causes) of autism will also have significance for the effective treatment and prevention of the disorder. Part III discusses treatment approaches and the related topic of follow-up studies of autistic individuals. Since beliefs about causation often influence treatment, an understanding of causal factors will help to assess and adjust the various approaches to treatment. Moreover, knowledge of such factors may aid in developing effective preventive measures.

Finally, a clear understanding of the cause of autism will let the parents of these children know where they stand. If it is caused primarily by certain damaging parental attitudes or faulty child-rearing methods, then the parents need to know specifically what they did wrong so that they can try to change in order to improve the autism in their child and prevent problems in future offspring. On the other hand, if it is determined primarily by organic factors, then these parents will have no need, as Rimland has said, "to suffer the shame, guilt, inconvenience, financial expense, and marital discord which so often accompany the assumption of psychogenic etiology" (7, p. 40).

To facilitate understanding of the different hypotheses concerning causation to be presented in the following chapters, it is necessary to first define more clearly the terms *biogenic* and *psychogenic* since they are central to the discussion.

With some behavioral and intellectual disorders there are definite organic causes—causes that take the form of a physical deficit or damage within the organism. The term biogenic is frequently used in referring to such causes. In mental retardation and other developmental disabilities, biogenic causes can be indicted with varying degrees of confidence. In some cases, as in Down's Syndrome or "mongolism," the retardation can be traced to a clearly defined genetic anomaly with highly specific effects (100). If we compare a Down's child from a Brahmin family in Boston with another Down's child from a sharecropper's family in Appalachia, the two will resemble each other more in physical, intellectual, and behavioral characteristics than they will their own siblings. Despite the likely differences in intellectual stimulation in their environments, the chances of either child's learning to work algebra problems or to parse complex sentences will be infinitesimal. In Down's Syndrome, then, we can clearly see the pervasive and limiting influence of one extra chromosome—a biogenic factor.

In most other biogenic forms of mental retardation the effects are not as precise as in Down's Syndrome, but they are still there (101). In some cases, the organic condition may exist, as in Down's Syndrome, before the child is born. Two such *prenatal* problems—phenylketonuria (PKU) and Rubella Syndrome—and how they relate to autism are considered in Chapter 9. In other cases, the condition may arise during the *perinatal* stage, that is, while the child is being born. The infant, for example, may sustain brain damage due to lack of oxygen associated with difficulties during delivery. Or in other cases, the damage may be *postnatal,* occurring well after the child is born. A three-year-old, for example, may suffer severe brain damage from lead intoxication after eating lead-based paint. The term biogenic, then, includes not only innate or congenital defects but also organic damage resulting from environmental trauma of a physical nature.

I have cited only a few examples of organic or biogenic conditions that may produce mental retardation or brain damage. The problems associated with these conditions, however, go beyond intellectual deficits or learning impairments. Brain-damaged children, whether they are retarded or of normal intelligence, often have communication disorders and significant behavioral difficulties that include hyperactivity, attention disorders, and poor impulse control (102).

Biogenic factors have also been shown to play a causal role in some severe emotional problems (103). The senile psychoses shown by some old people is associated with the hardening of the arteries that occurs with advanced age. The deranged behavior demonstrated by Al Capone in his last years was due to paresis, the final stages of syphilitic invasion of the brain.

Some disorders of childhood (such as Heller's disease and PKU) once thought to be emotional disturbances induced by social factors were later shown to have an organic basis. The disordered behavior and lack of physical stigmata in children with such diseases can be quite misleading. Many a medical student has prematurely attributed the psychotic behavior of a PKU child to psychogenic factors before learning of the actual diagnosis.

In mental retardation and behavior disorders that have no demonstrable organic basis, the causal relationships become harder to pinpoint. In the majority of cases of mild retardation, no definite biological cause can be determined, although there may be suspected contributory factors such as nutritional deficits and inadequate prenatal health care (100). There is little doubt that environmental deprivation during early life can hinder intellectual development and contribute to retardation of this type. A child from a severely deprived social and intellectual environment may be mildly retarded at three, but with a change to a more stimulating, enriched environment, he may be functioning as a normal child at five.

Environmental or social causes in some behavioral or emotional disorders of childhood can be pointed to with some confidence. A child may show an emotional reaction to a clearly specifiable situation; when the situation is changed, the emotional problem diminishes or disappears. A phobia, or an irrational fear, is a good example. A child may become hysterical at the sight of any dog, even a friendly puppy, because of an unpleasant past experience with one dog. When not around dogs, the child may be normal in every respect. I could cite other examples, such as adjustment reactions, in which the cause of an emotional or behavioral problem appears to reside in the environment.

With many chronic and severe emotional disorders of childhood, a clear indictment cannot be made of causal agents either within the organism or in the social environment, and here is where speculation begets controversy. When classified according to cause, these disorders can be labeled either as *functional* or *psychogenic*. With the term *functional* we admit our current ignorance of the cause and say we do not know; with the term *psychogenic* we assert that the cause is psychological rather than organic. In calling a disorder psychogenic we presume, then, that it has no physical basis but instead is caused by adverse influences in the psychosocial environment in which the person lives; these influences consist mainly of interactions with other people.

Most advocates of a psychogenic basis for severe emotional disorders, such as Bruno Bettelheim (104), maintain that the social interaction most crucial to the emotional development of the child is the early relationship with the mother (or mother-figure). Hardly anyone questions the importance of this relationship; but some, such as the British psychiatrist Michael Rutter (105), think that its significance has been greatly exaggerated in speculations on the development of certain childhood disorders. The terms "maternal deprivation" and "maternal rejection" have become shibboleths, authoritatively invoked to explain any problem the child may have, and the mother often has found herself the unwitting culprit in disorders ranging from thumbsucking to bedwetting to autism.

The issue of psychogenesis versus biogenesis is the recurrent theme of the controversial questions considered in Part II. Since the parents have from the beginning figured prominently in the controversy over the cause of autism, I start with them in Chapter 6, reviewing the research on their intellectual, social, and emotional characteristics. Chapter 7 examines some of the psychogenic hypotheses that relate autism to these parental characteristics and child-rearing practices. Chapter 8 considers the other side of the argument, summarizing some of the major biogenic theories, and Chapter 9 includes inferences and insights drawn from research findings that bear on these hypotheses about the basic nature and cause of autism.

To dissolve any false expectations, it should be reiterated that research has yet to uncover the cause or causes of autism. The evolution of professional thinking revealed in the next few chapters should attest to the dangers of jumping to premature conclusions. Still I hope that the material presented reflects the progress that has been made toward a better understanding of the disorder.

6 Parents and Family

Sometimes I even think that Noah is my own insanity walking, my cursed other-self inflicted upon my own second son. . . .

But his is a world I am shut out from, mine is a world he has been unable to enter. He still spends most of his days in happy withdrawal, often smiling as if at some inner joke, as he makes the rounds of our house, always almost symbolically closing each door behind him. But then there are also days and nights when he has sudden fits of sadness that are uncontrollable and unbearable, as he writhes upon the floor or in his bed in utter and abject unhappiness. . . .

But I still don't know exactly what's wrong with Noah. I only know something is profoundly wrong with him. . . . I also know I must try not to feel more sorry for myself than for Noah, but some days I forget. (9, pp. 78, 90-93)

The poignant guilt and discouragement expressed by Josh Greenfeld in his book *A Child Called Noah* (9) probably is shared by most parents of autistic children. To add to the emotional burden of coping with an autistic child, many of these parents have had their feelings intensified by the professionals from whom they seek help. Many have gone from one specialist to another (in professional circles this is disdainfully called "shopping") to be bedazzled by a hodgepodge of such labels as "mentally retarded," "emotionally disturbed," "brain-damaged," "aphasic," or "atypical," the label at the moment being determined by the predilection of the particular specialist. Then, when their child is finally diagnosed as autistic, they naturally want professional help in understanding the problem and assuring that the child gets the most effective treatment program.

Instead of finding a sympathetic ear, however, the parents often have been confronted with a quizzical eyebrow or indicting finger. As parents of an autistic child, they have found themselves the victims of certain a priori assumptions held by many professionals—assumptions about causation of emotional disorders and, more personally, assumptions about their own personality and its critical role in the development of autism. These parents have discovered that many professionals tend to assume automatically that if a disorder is "emotional," then it is invariably the result of a defective social environment, particularly the environment provided by the mother in the first years of the child's life. Further, they may assume that all parents of autistic children represent in classic form the cold, rejecting, intellectual parent who is the primary causal agent in the child's profound disturbance.

Later chapters point out that these assumptions about the parental role in the cause of autism may be based more on preconceived notions and hasty conclusions than on careful interpretation of available findings. This chapter considers some of the parental and family features that at first glance may lead to these preconceptions.

Before the more controversial findings about parents of autistic children are reviewed, a few other facts about the family should be mentioned. Although Kanner (106) reported a disproportionate number of autistic children from Jewish or Anglo-Saxon families, later studies have shown that autism occurs in families of all ethnic groups around the world (3). Males appear to be especially vulnerable to the disorder, being affected three to five times more frequently than females (4, 6). Unlike other severe mental disorders, autism does not run in families. The parents and blood relatives of autistic children show an extremely low incidence of mental illness (3, 7, 64). Furthermore, autistic children do not appear to be the products of broken homes since divorce and separation is uncommon among their parents (7). Most live with their own parents rather than with adoptive or foster parents.

Because of their significance in theories of the cause of autism, the parents have been the subject of almost as much study and controversy as the children themselves. Most of this research has centered on two basic questions: Do parents of autistic children constitute a special and homogeneous group with regard to intellectual and personality characteristics? If so, how do these characteristics relate to the development of autism in their child?

Kanner's Studies of Parents

In his original paper and subsequent articles Kanner (e.g., 1, 16, 106) argued that these parents are indeed a very special group in both intelligence and personality. He noted first that a vast majority of the parents studied by him and his colleagues have been of very high intellectual, educational, and occupational status. His description of the parents of the original eleven children illustrated this point:

> Four fathers are psychiatrists, one is a brilliant lawyer, one a chemist and law school graduate employed in the Government Patent Office, one a plant pathologist, one a professor of forestry, one an advertising copy writer who has a degree in law and has studied in three universities, one is a mining engineer and one a successful business man.
>
> Nine of eleven mothers are college graduates. Of the two who have only high school eduation, one was a secretary in a pathology laboratory, and the other ran a theatrical booking office in New York City before marriage. Among the others, there was a free lance writer, a physician, a psychologist, a graduate nurse, and Frederick's mother was successively a purchasing agent, the director of secretarial studies in a girls' school, and a teacher of history.
>
> Among the grandparents and collaterals there are many physicians, scientists, writers, journalists, and students of art. All but three of the families are represented either in *Who's Who in America* or in *American Men of Science,* or in both. (1, p. 248)

Kanner noted secondly that these parents, along with their extremely high intellectual accomplishments, had certain personality traits in common. He described them as being obsessive, cold, detached, and reserved in expression of affection:

> One other fact stands out prominently. In the whole group, there are very few really warmhearted fathers and mothers. For the most part,

the parents, grandparents, and collaterals are persons strongly preoccupied with abstractions of a scientific, literary, or artistic nature, and
limited in genuine interest in people. Even some of the happiest mar-
riages are rather cold and formal affairs. (1, p. 250)

By 1954, Kanner had collected statistics on the first hundred sets
of parents of autistic children studied at his clinic. These statistics
were quite consistent with the features of the original parents, showing
much higher intellectual, educational, and occupational attainment
than is found on the average in parents of nonautistic children. These
parents were described by Kanner as "indisputably intelligent, functioning in society "at the top of scientific, artistic, and commercial
enterprises."

These parents, according to Kanner, were also similar in personality characteristics to the original group. In *Time* (107) he depicted
them as "highly organized, professional parents, cold and rational,"
who "just happened to defrost long enough to produce a child." He
stressed, however, that the children were not rejected or ignored in
the usual sense. In most cases, he found the mothers to be meticulous
in attending to the needs of the children: "They were anxious to do
a good job, and this meant mechanized service of the kind which is
rendered by an overconscientious gasoline station attendant" (16,
p. 424).

Eisenberg's Study of Fathers

In 1957 Leon Eisenberg, Kanner's colleague and former student,
reported a study of the personality characteristics of the one-hundred
fathers in this group of parents (108). He stated that eighty-five of
these fathers showed the typical personality pattern—that is, they
were "obsessive, detached, humorless individuals" who were "perfec-
tionistic to an extreme" and "preoccupied with detailed minutiae to
the exclusion of concern for over-all meaning." They also showed "a
capacity for concentration on their own pursuits amidst veritable chaos
about them" (p. 721). One of the fathers, for example, stated that his
power of concentration was like that of his father, who had continued
to write a manuscript while trapped in a wrecked railroad car tilted
twenty degrees from the vertical. These fathers, according to Eisenberg, appeared to have children, not because they wanted them, but

because they considered children to be a formal obligation of marriage.

In the article, Eisenberg presented vignettes of three fathers who exemplified these typical characteristics. One was a caricature of the highly competent, precise, machinelike surgeon who "dealt with infected gall bladders, diseased bowels, or tumors, with little or no curiosity about the person in whom these anatomical problems were housed" (p. 717). Another was a very bright accountant who spent his evenings reading everything from mathematical treatises to trash, almost totally ignoring his family. The third was a bacteriologist whose sole concern for his son Billy was to prevent infection; this necessitated keeping Billy almost completely isolated from human contact, since the father viewed human beings primarily as purveyors of bacteria. Eisenberg pointed out that fifteen of the one-hundred fathers in the study did not fit the typical pattern. Further, he reported that almost all of the 131 siblings of the autistic children were normal in emotional development. These findings are crucial in assessing the parental influence in the development of autism.

In summarizing his analysis, Eisenberg stated that these fathers have "serious personality difficulties" that greatly interfere with their fulfilling the normal paternal role; further, these problems seriously affect the pattern of family life in a harmful way. Eisenberg suggested that his findings pointed to a need to reconsider the pat theory that the autistic child's disorder is caused by maternal inadequacies alone. He pointed out, too, that the presence of normal children in these same families suggests that other factors, possibly within the child, may play a role in the development of the psychosis.

Other Studies of Parents

Kanner's and Eisenberg's contention that the parents of autistic children constitute a special group has stimulated a great deal of further research and discussion. One of the most thorough reviews of the research and literature that bear on this issue was done by Bernard Rimland in his book *Infantile Autism*, published in 1964. Rimland included in his analysis the work of W. R. Keeler, who did a detailed and objective appraisal of the parents' intelligence. Keeler (109) reported that the parents had IQs too high to be assessed with currently available tests. After looking carefully at virtually all of the reports on autism available at the time, Rimland concluded that the "evidence overwhelmingly supports Kanner's unprecedented early report that the parents of autistic children form a unique and highly homogeneous group in terms of intellect and personality" (7, p. 38).

The issue, however, is still unsettled since research reports published since Rimland's review do not consistently support his conclusion, especially with regard to parental personality. Further, questions have been raised about the particular group of parents which were included in the early studies and upon which the conclusions were based. Some writers have proposed, for example, that the early statistics indicating extremely high parental intelligence may have been based on a select sample of parents; that is, those parents who were attuned to behavior and language problems and sought psychiatric help, especially at Johns Hopkins, tended to be wealthier, better educated, and brighter than most parents in the general population. The autistic children of less sophisticated parents, then, may have gone undetected.

A recent study by Eric Schopler, Carol Andrews, and Karen Strupp (110) suggests that the early studies were indeed dealing with a select sample of well-to-do parents and that autistic children may be just as prevalent among families of lower social status. After finding no significant social class differences in the families of 522 autistic children evaluated at the University of North Carolina at Chapel Hill between 1966 and 1976, these researchers concluded that more and more autistic children from lower socioeconomic families will be seen with the increasing availability and publicity of services.

These statistics on parental and family characteristics are further complicated by the tendency among professionals in recent years to use a less stringent definition of autism. While the early studies may have dealt with too narrow a sample, some of the recent studies may have considered too broad a sample, including children who fail to· meet the original diagnostic critieria delineated by Kanner.

In a comprehensive review of all the research on family factors in autism, William McAcdoo and Marian DeMyer (111) of the Indiana University School of Medicine gleaned some general conclusions from the diverse findings. They concluded that parents of autistic children, in comparison to parents of children with other behavioral disorders or handicaps, come from more affluent homes and that the heads of household are better educated and have higher IQs. They pointed out, however, that these differences cannot necessarily be related to the cause of autism since other unknown or uncontrolled variables such as bias in patient selection may be operating. These authors also concluded that research reveals no more signs of mental illness in parents of autistic children than can be found in parents of children with nonpsychotic organic disorders or nonpsychotic emotional disorders. Further, parents of autistic children show "significantly less psychopathology" than do parents who are being treated in psychiatric outpatient clinics; as a whole they demonstrate "no extreme personality traits such as coldness, obsessiveness, social anxiety, or extreme rage" and "no specific defects in acceptance, nurturing, warmth, feeding, and tactile and general stimulation of their infants . . ." (p. 165). Finally, McAdoo and DeMyer stated that the confusion and uncertainty exhibited by most parents in raising their autistic child "may result from the stress of trying unsuccessfully to understand and influence a child with a neurobiologically based defect in both verbal and nonverbal communication" (p. 165). The severe and persistent stress resulting from this situation may produce parental changes in personality and potentially threaten the marriage.

General Conclusions Regarding Parental Intelligence and Personality

Looking at all of the reported research, it seems fair to say that parents of carefully diagnosed autistic children are generally, though not exclusively, of above average intelligence and socioeconomic status; many reported in the literature are outstanding in their intellectual, educational, and occupational accomplishments. As the English psychiatrist Lorna Wing (112) has suggested, the classically autistic children, as defined by Kanner, are more likely to have such parents than the less typical, more retarded children. However, with more and more community services available, there may be an increasing number of classically autistic children whose parents fail to fit the original picture.

It is notable that the number of articles and books written by parents of autistic children appears to be disproportionately higher than the number written by parents of children with other more prevalent disorders (e.g., 9, 10, 11, 113, 114). In the absence of any formal research, however, this can be offered only as a plausible hypothesis. Aside from providing vivid descriptions of autistic behavior and firsthand accounts of the frustrations of coping with an autistic child, these parents have offered some of the most perceptive and sophisticated insights into the basic defects and possible causes of autism. The quantity and quality of these writings lends informal support to the conclusion that parents of autistic children are often intellectually superior individuals.

In view of the findings on the intellectual characteristics of these parents, a reasonable assumption is that the islets of brightness reported in the classically autistic children may indeed be vestiges of a superior intellectual strain—vestiges that rarely materialize into the productive abilities shown by the parents (4). We wonder what the potential of some of these children might have been if the autism had been averted.

The results of the studies of the personality traits of these parents are harder to evaluate because such traits cannot be assessed as precisely and objectively as intellectual factors. The recent findings strongly indicate, though, that the percent of parents with the so-called "typical" personality pattern described by Kanner and his associates is much lower than earlier studies indicated. In fact, more and more evidence supports the notion that these parents, as a group, are no different in emotional characteristics than parents of normal children or handicapped children with no emotional disorders.

Nevertheless, the assumption that these parents are pathogenic underlies the theories of causation discussed in the next chapter—theories that still influence the attitudes of many lay and professional persons who have contact with parents of autistic children. The presumed cause, however, may likely be the effect. Rather than being cold, aloof, and rejecting, the mother may be naturally perplexed, frustrated, and guiltridden over her failure to reach an unresponsive child. It is no wonder that she may appear confused, defensive, and even angry in the presence of professional eyes that may be programmed to see her as a causal agent for her child's profound disturbance.

7 Psychogenic Hypotheses

The infant, because of pain or discomfort and the anxiety they cause, or because he misreads the mother's actions or feelings, or correctly assesses her negative feelings, may retreat from her and the world. The mother, for her part, either frustrated in her motherly feelings, or out of her own anxiety, may respond not with gentle pursuit, but with anger or injured indifference. This is apt to create new anxiety in the child, to which may now be added the feeling that the world (as represented by the mother) not only causes anxiety but is also angry or indifferent as the case may be. (104, p. 72)

In his book *The Empty Fortress* (104), Bruno Bettelheim, director of the Orthogenic School of the University of Chicago, proposed that autism is precipitated by the mother's wish, either conscious or unconscious, that her child did not exist. Bettelheim's hypothesis, which is considered in more detail shortly, represents perhaps the most radical position among psychogenic theories. All of these theories share the common assumption that adverse influences in the infant's psychological environment engender, or at least precipitate, the autistic disorder. These presumed influences are tied to the atypical personality patterns and child-rearing attitudes of the parents as reported in the early studies. As noted in the previous chapter, Kanner (1, 16) and Eisenberg (108) described the parents as highly intelligent but obsessive, cold, detached, and reserved in expression of affection. Although

74

Kanner himself has been reluctant to do so, the psychogenic theorists have ascribed a causal role to these reported parental characteristics. These theorists generally assume that the autistic child is potentially normal at birth but becomes abnormal because of these parental influences. Autism is viewed, then, as extreme emotional reaction to the abnormal psychological atmosphere provided by the parents.

Bettelheim's Psychogenic Theory

The psychogenic theory that has received the most publicity and evoked perhaps the most controversy is that of Bettelheim (104). As previously mentioned, Bettelheim has proposed that autism is triggered by the mother's wish that the child did not exist. The child senses at a very early age this basic rejection by the mother and erects defenses against the destructive designs of the mother. These barriers, in turn, prevent the development of the child's "self" or "ego." According to the psychoanalytic view of personality development, which Bettelheim subscribes to, the normal child's "self" or "ego" crystallizes through interaction with other people, primarily the mother during the early years. Since the autistic child does not interact, his "self" does not emerge. So he builds an "empty fortress"—a defensive structure against the perceived destructive force of the mother, a structure in which no "self" resides.

All of the autistic symptoms, according to Bettelheim, reflect the child's concerted attempt to ward off an intrusion by an environment perceived as hostile; they also serve to deny the existence of his "self." This relentless defense against social interaction and this negation of selfhood is revealed clearly in the child's perplexing use of language. His reversal of pronouns is significant, not because he reverses them but because he shuns pronouns that directly refer to himself. He uses the pronoun "you" while avoiding the pronoun "I," thereby acknowledging the selfhood of others but denying his own. Similarly he uses the word "No" but refrains from saying "Yes;" this signifies his "extreme and deliberate negativism"—his "total refusal to get involved with the world" (p. 428).

Bettelheim stated that autistic children, with their language, "pose us riddles to solve, and test our desire to understand them, a desire that would also attest to our willingness that they should exist" (p. 430). The delayed echoes, repeated over and over, have "deep meaning" if probed enough. Bettelheim cited as an example the case of Marcia, the nonspeaking daughter of an English-born woman. Day after day, Marcia sang the lines from the musical "My Fair Lady," "Why don't the English teach their children to speak?"

Though Bettelheim thinks that autism is basically a psychogenic disorder, he does not categorically preclude an organic predisposition. In an interview in *Psychology Today* (115), he stated: "It serves no purpose to make parents of autistic children feel guilty. While their attitudes and handling of their child might have precipitated the autism, that by itself is not a sufficient cause. It is even possible that they handled the child as they did because of his unusual responses to them. And perhaps another child, handled in the same way, would not have become autistic" (p. 22). Even if an organic predisposition exists, Bettelheim still maintains that the precipitating factor in autism is the parents' reaction to the child, especially the mother's rejection of the child.

A Parent's Reaction to Bettelheim

Bettelheim may have offered his views in a theoretical and impersonal manner, but parents often take them very personally. In an article entitled "The View from the Couch" in the *Journal of Child Psychology and Psychiatry*, Frances Eberhardy (116), the mother of an autistic child, expressed her reaction:

> A magazine article on Dr. Bettelheim's . . . latest book was shown to me, since my own son was once an "empty fortress." The reporter's first paragraph was as biting as a Wisconsin blizzard. "For the withdrawn and psychotic child, the yellow door (of the Orthogenic School) is their first experience with warmth and brightness."
>
> Dr. Bettelheim's own words proved to be no more comforting. "The precipitating factor in infantile autism is the parent's wish that his child should not exist."
>
> I am willing to take Dr. Bettelheim's words that he has seen parents who wish that their child should not exist, or mothers like the one who told him she "thought of him (her son) as a thing rather than a person;" but in the seven years I have been active in a parent group for emotionally disturbed children, I have met no such parent. (p. 257)

Mrs. Eberhardy continued in this article to make a plea to professionals to show more concern and less condemnation toward parents who are quite confused and guilt-ridden over their role in the development of the child's autism.

Tinbergen's Position

Parents like Mrs. Eberhardy are not the only ones to voice strong objection to Bettelheim's psychogenic views. In the next chapter, a number of scholars and scientists take issue with his position. One prominent scientist, however, who has recently espoused some of Bettelheim's ideas is Nicolaas Tinbergen (74), the Nobel Prize-winning ethologist. At first glance, Bettelheim and Tinbergen appear to be strange theoretical bedfellows—Bettelheim the psychoanalytic clinician who makes inferences about the autistic child's psyche and Tinbergen the biologist who meticulously observes the behavior patterns of animals and emphasizes the inborn nature of these patterns. Despite the differences in background and approach, they both agree that autism is basically an emotional disorder induced by the social environment.

Tinbergen and his wife Elisabeth only recently have directed their study toward the bewildering behavior of the autistic child. For over forty years, they have studied the behavior of various animal species and published fascinating papers on such diverse topics as homing in the digger wasp, mating in the stickleback fish, courtship of the Grayling butterfly, eggshell removal by the black-headed gull, and food-hoarding in the fox (117, 118). The Tinbergens believed that the ethologist's basic techniques of "watching and wondering" about the behavior of animals in their natural habitat might also be applied to the behavior of autistic children; such observation, they thought, might yield some clues to a better understanding of the disorder (74).

They started with the notion that much could be learned about autistic children by studying their nonverbal behavior and comparing it with the nonverbal behavior of normal children. They noted that normal children in certain situations, such as in the presence of strangers, do indeed show some "autistic" characteristics. For example, they keep a certain distance, maintain a serious facial expression, avoid eye contact, and assume unusual postures. A normal child shows these "passing attacks" of autistic behavior in situations that engender a conflict between two competing motivations. A shy four-year-old, for example, may be called to join in a group activity on his first day in nursery school. The situation may evoke in him negative or fearful responses—a tendency to withdraw both physically and mentally; at the same time, the situation may encourage him toward positive social and exploratory behavior. If the fear prevails in this conflictual situation, the child may draw away from the group, maintain a "distant" expression, and avoid looking at the faces of the children. Children who are naturally timid, Tinbergen said, show these bouts of autistic behavior more readily than children who are more confident. But he stressed that they all respond to the environment.

The Tinbergens discovered that with certain "taming procedures," these autistic episodes in normal children could be eliminated. They found, too, that these procedures worked in drawing some severely autistic children "out of their shell." These findings led Tinbergen (74) to conclude that many autistic children are "potentially normal children, whose affiliative and subsequent socialization processes have gone wrong in one way or another" (p. 22). He also believed that the problems "can often be traced back to something in the early environment—on occasion a frightening accident, but most often something in the behavior of the parents, in particular the mother" (p. 22). He stated that these parents frequently appear "to have been simply inexperienced (hence perhaps the high incidence among firstborns); or overapprehensive; or overefficient and intrusive; or, perhaps most often, they are people who are themselves under stress" (p. 22). He emphasized that the unfortunate parents should not be blamed since they are the victims of stress and deserve as much compassion, and perhaps as much help, as the children themselves.

Tinbergen thinks, then, that autism is primarily an emotional disturbance, a severe anxiety reaction, which "prevents or retards normal affiliation and subsequent socialization." The language deficits and lack of exploratory behavior are secondary to this basic disturbance which, according to Tinbergen, is caused neither by genetic anomalies nor gross brain damage but by early environmental conditions. He considers most autistic children and their parents to be "genuine victims of environmental stress."

Tinbergen has stated that if his position is incorrect, "the outlook for a real cure for these children would of course be bleak, for the best one one could hope for would be an amelioration of their suffering" (p. 20). Like Bettelheim, he thinks that treatment should be done "at an emotional level" and directed toward the reduction of the child's anxiety. A later chapter reviews Bettelheim's method of treatment as well as a treatment approach more directly related to the views of Tinbergen and other ethologists.

Ferster's Operant Learning Theory

Another view of autism that we should consider before turning to biogenic theories is one based on the learning principles of behaviorism. This view differs radically from the psychodynamic formulations of Bettelheim but still attributes autism to social environmental influences. While Bettelheim's theory is steeped in the clinical tradition of Freudian psychology, behaviorism is based on the rigorous experimental tradition of Pavlov and Skinner. The behaviorist makes no inferences about what is going on "inside the mind" of the child; rather, he studies the child's overt behavior as a function of the child's environment.

According to the behaviorist, the child's social behavior is shaped to a large extent by the consequences provided by other people. These consequences generally are of two types, positive or negative. Positive consequences accelerate or maintain the behavior that they follow and may take the form of primary reinforcers or secondary reinforcers. Primary reinforcers are natural rewards that reduce some physiological drive such as hunger; secondary reinforcers are stimuli that initially have no reward value but assume such value through association with primary reinforcers. Food, of course, is a powerful primary reinforcer for most young children; as they grow older, however, they learn to repond more and more to secondary reinforcers such as praise, smiles, and other forms of positive attention.

Negative consequences include direct punishment (aversive stimulation) or the withholding or withdrawal of positive consequences. Like positive consequences, negative consequences can be primary or secondary. A parent, for example, can punish a child with a sharp spank on the rear or a sharp reprimand; or he can withhold from the child a cookie or a smile of approval. As a general rule, punishment is not the most effective means of eliminating unacceptable behavior in the child. When followed by punishment the behavior in question usually is temporarily suppressed although not necessarily eliminated. When consistently followed by the absence of positive consequences, the behavior generally diminishes and finally disappears. According to learning theorists, the best combination for parents to use in the long-range shaping of behavior is positive reinforcement of appropriate behavior and withdrawal of such reinforcement for inappropriate behavior. Research reviewed in a later chapter indicates, however, that punishment may be the most direct and effective means of controlling certain types of behavior in the autistic child.

Applying these principles to the development of social behavior in children, the learning theorist says that the basic social responsiveness of newborn babies is shaped by primary rewards. The infant learns to associate the sight and touch of his mother with warm milk (which reduces his hunger) and a dry diaper (which reduces his discomfort). Through this pairing with primary reinforcers, the mother herself and the stimuli associated with her presence become secondary or social reinforcers to which the child responds positively. The mother's attention, then, becomes in itself a powerful reinforcer for the learning of further social behavior. Some learning theorists think that the autistic child's basic problem is that he fails to acquire these social reinforcers. Some attribute this failure at least in part to a defect present at birth. Others, however, such as the experimental psychologist C. B. Ferster (119, 120), propose that the autistic child's failure to develop appropriate social behavior is due primarily to environmental influences, particularly those exerted by the mother in her selective reinforcement of certain behavior patterns in the child.

Ferster's theory exemplifies the application of operant learning principles to an analysis of the behavior of the autistic child. Ferster started with the well-established finding that a child's environment can have a very powerful influence on his behavioral development. He cited cases of children who have been kept locked in closets or other highly restrictive environments during most of their early years. These children often become "primitive" and "animal-like" in their behavior. When placed in another environment with consequences arranged carefully for them, these children can learn new, more appropriate forms of behavior. A radical change in environment can therefore bring about a radical change in their behavior. Ferster thinks that it makes sense, then, to study carefully the surroundings of the autistic child for circumstances that may explain the gross deficiencies in his behavior.

Ferster (120) has stated that the difference between the autistic child and the normal child is not in the type of behavior shown but in the frequency of the behavior. The normal child occasionally shows withdrawn, self-stimulatory, and atavistic behaviors; the autistic child shows those behaviors intensely and consistently. Further, "the past experiences of the autistic child differ from those of the normal child not so much in *kind* as in *intensity* and *frequency*" (p. 35). Since he observed that the evidence for biological causation is meager, Ferster proposed that the limited behavioral repertoire of the autistic child has developed because of these differences in reinforcement history; the key figures in the child's early reinforcement history are, of course, his parents.

Ferster speculated that these parents, because of their preoccupation with other matters, regard taking care of the child as aversive and intrusive; they therefore fail to reward appropriate, effective social behaviors, and at the same time they reinforce a restricted range of inappropriate behaviors—behaviors that usually have small, limited effects on the child's physical environment. Appropriate behaviors that have more effect on the environment, such as handling or moving household objects or playing appropriately with toys, may be prevented or suppressed because they intrude more on the parents' environment; but inappropriate behaviors that have less effect on the environment, and are less bother to the parents, such as rocking, hand-flapping, or twirling a jar lid, may be allowed to continue and are subtly reinforced. When the behavior reaches severe proportions, such as when the child bashes his head against a wall, it results in a great deal of attention and solicitude from the parents and thereby is reinforced. So a vicious circle emerges, with socially appropriate behaviors being diminished and extinguished and a limited number of socially inappropriate, maladaptive behaviors increasingly being reinforced and sustained. When the child reaches four or five years of age and enters the broader social world of nursery school or kindergarten, the cumulative effects of the reinforcement history are shown in behavior patterns that are firmly entrenched and difficult to eliminate. Since he shows none of the age appropriate behaviors that the kindergarten teacher reserves her reinforcement for, the circle continues.

In order to break the cycle, Ferster thinks that a carefully controlled environment has to be arranged for the child—an environment that

eliminates the inappropriate behaviors and reinforces appropriate behaviors in systematic fashion. Such is the approach of behavior modification, a treatment technique that is considered in a later chapter.
The results of behavior modification with autistic children suggest that
Ferster's theory has its limits and that the basic defects in these children
cannot be explained solely through learning history.

Interaction Theories

Thus far, the reviewed theories have ascribed autism to influences
in the social environment. Bettelheim, Tinbergen, and Ferster, despite
differences in their approach to the study of autism, all agree that the
causes are more environmental than organic. Other theorists (e.g.,
20, 53, 121) propose that autism cannot be clearly attributed to either
psychogenic factors or biogenic ones but rather to a combination or
interaction of the two. Some invoke the concept of the "critical
period," a term derived from the fascinating animal research of Konrad
Lorenz, the noted ethologist. Lorenz (122) and other researchers have
shown that certain animals, especially geese, ducks, and other fowl,
go through a critical period in their early development during which
they are most susceptible to forming basic social attachments. If the
opportunity for forming appropriate social attachments is missing, then
the animal may form inappropriate attachments or suffer a lifelong
defect in socialization.

Although it remains to be clearly demonstrated, some theorists
(e.g., 123) think that there may be a similar critical period in human
infancy—a period when the child is most ready to learn basic social
responses and form a primary attachment bond with a mother-figure.
If something in the child's social environment goes wrong or is missing
during this period, then he may fail to develop appropriate social and
emotional responsiveness.

Some interactionist theorists (e.g., 53, 121) think that autism is
precipitated in children who are genetically more vulnerable during
this critical period to parental stress, neglect, or rejection and other
social trauma; other children with stronger genetic resistance to these
social influences survive the critical period without developing autism.
Bettelheim and Tinbergen probably go along to some degree with this
view but consider the environmental influences to be overriding.

Kanner himself appears to favor the view that autism is an affective disorder that results from both organic and psychosocial influences. He seems, however, to give more weight to the organic influences. As noted earlier, he concluded his original article (1) with the statement that the eleven children appeared to have "inborn autistic disturbances of affective contact." In his later articles, though, he developed the thesis that the basic disturbance, though inherited from the parents, may be exacerbated by the unusual environment provided by the parents (124).

In an article entitled "Early Infantile Autism Revisited," Kanner (124) summed up his position by saying that "autism is not primarily an acquired, or 'man-made' disease." He stated that although the parents have been found to be "rather detached people," no direct cause-and-effect relationship can be drawn. "Making parents feel guilty of responsibility for their child's autism," he wrote, "is not only erroneous, but cruelly adds insult to injury" (p. 139).

A later chapter reviews the evidence that has led Kanner and others to believe that a strict psychogenic view of autism is invalid. Before looking at this evidence, however, we should examine some of the biogenic theories.

8 Biogenic Hypotheses

There are two major theories relating to the treatment of children with severe behavior disorders. These theories are in sharp conflict, and their implications are very pervasive, since they relate not only to how to remedy the problem, but to what originally caused the disorder, how it could be prevented, and what the outcome will be. Now for reasons which I've never really understood—and maybe the chief reason is just plain fuzzy thinking on the part of those who hold this position—many people, including quite a few educators, seem to feel the two competing theories aren't really in competition. They say (often rather smugly), that there must be some truth on each side of the argument, and that the ultimate answer will inevitably be found somewhere in the middle. That may be so, but I doubt it. I'm sure that in Columbus' day there were "eclectics" who tried to avoid controversy by insisting that the earth could be neither round nor flat—that because there was disagreement, the earth's shape must logically be somewhere in between, perhaps like a marshmallow that had been sat on, or an oversized M & M. Their descendants are still with us. (125, p. 33)

The psychologist Bernard Rimland makes no bones about where he stands on the nature-nurture controversy over autism; he objects to the interactionist or "middle-ground" theories almost as strongly as he does to the psychogenic ones. Himself the father of an autistic son and the founder of the National Society for Autistic Children, Rimland has had both personal and professional involvement with the problem of autism. His book *Infantile Autism* (7), which won the 1962 Century Psychology Series Award, is still regarded as one of the most thorough reviews of the clinical and experimental literature on autism. It also represents one of the most cogent (and iconoclastic) arguments that has yet been written against the psychogenic position.

Rimland admits that when he embarked on his study of autism, he thought that it was a psychogenic disorder. After an exhaustive review and analysis of the literature, however, he concluded that autism is basically a biogenic disorder, and he offers a theory of causation that he thinks is consistent with research findings.

In contrast to psychogenic theorists like Bettelheim who think that autism is primarily an emotional or "affective" disturbance, Rimland proposes that autism is basically a cognitive and perceptual disorder with secondary emotional components. Since cognitive and perceptual functions are central to Rimland's and other theories discussed in this chapter, it may be helpful to define these and related functions before going further.

Sensory, Perceptual, and Cognitive Functions

The discussion refers to the diagram on the opposite page in defining these psychological functions and how they relate to one another. The diagram, of course, is an oversimplification of extremely complex processes that are far from being understood. The three main functional components—*sensory, perceptual,* and *cognitive*—are not directly observable in the developing child; we can only infer them from his response output in relation to stimulus input. They may be viewed as three different, though interrelated and overlapping, systems that process stimuli coming from both outside and within the child. Each component represents a different level of neural development and activity, with sensory functions being the lowest (and the first to develop) and cognitive functions being the highest (and the last to develop). Each can be related to brain anatomy with varying degrees of precision, with sensory functions being more specifically localized than perceptual or cognitive functions.

The sensory component, of course, includes the reception of stimuli through the eyes, ears, and other sense organs. This stimulation may come from outside the child, such as the touch of the mother or

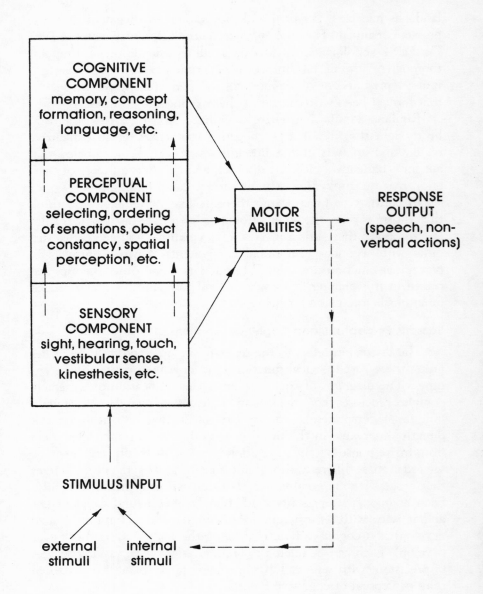

**DIAGRAM OF BASIC PSYCHOLOGICAL FUNCTIONS
AND THEIR INTERRELATIONS**

the sound of a telephone ringing, or from within the child, such as the sensation of movement when the child rocks himself or turns his head. The normal newborn infant may at first experience this raw input as "one great blooming, buzzing confusion," but not for long. In a short time he begins to impose order on this welter of stimuli, selectively attending to some and ignoring others, and he begins to assign meaning to his sensations; he begins to "make some sense" of them. Even within the first month he begins to respond selectively to patterns and to the human face (126). This organization, selection, and "making sense" of sensations is generally called perception and is represented in the perceptual component in the diagram. Many types of perception—for example, form and pattern perception, depth perception, and figure-ground perception—appear to be innate and largely determined by neurological maturation in the child (126, 127, 128). Although some aspects of perception are shaped by his individual experiences in the world, many of the child's basic perceptual abilities seem to be "wired in" and present from birth.

One aspect of perceptual functioning that is especially relevant to one of the theories of autism that is discussed shortly is *perceptual constancy*. This refers to the tendency we have to perceive objects in the environment as constant despite variations in the way we experience them from time to time. *Size constancy* refers to our ability to perceive an object as the same object even though it actually looks smaller the farther it is from our eyes. Similarly, *shape constancy* refers to our ability to perceive an object as having the same shape even though the object is seen from differen angles and actually appears on our retina as different shapes. For example, if you close this book and hold it at various angles and distances, you would constantly perceive it as the same book with the same size and shape although the actual visual image on your retina is changing. With perceptual constancy, then, you are going a step beyond mere sensation. Further, your ability to recognize the book later as the same book, when it is lying on the desk across the room, is dependent on your facility for size and shape constancy.

Both size and shape constancy contribute to *object constancy*, which allows us to tie our present experience to past experiences. These perceptual constancies, which appear to develop in infancy in the normal child (129, 130) and which we take for granted in our everyday lives, may play a significant role in our understanding of some of the basic problems shown in the autistic child.

The cognitive or "thinking" functions include the storing of sensations and perceptions and the drawing of relationships among them in the form of concepts or ideas. In order to develop a "concept" or generalize, the child must be able to recognize common elements in different experiences; this usually requires that he relate the situation at hand to his memories of similar situations. When he applies the concept "hat" to a bonnet at one time and to a sombrero at another, he probably has learned that both are worn on the head. Many theorists agree that this ability to form concepts by relating present experience to past experience is severely impaired in the autistic child.

His impairment, however, appears to extend to other areas of cognition or thinking, and in understanding his disabilities we need first to know something of the normal child's abilities in these areas. The Swiss psychologist Jean Piaget has contributed greatly to our understanding of the normal child's development of cognitive functions. From his research Piaget has concluded that the child, as he grows from infancy to adulthood, progresses in his cognitive skills from primitive sensorimotor activities to high-level abstract thinking that includes not only concept formation but reasoning (131). The child proceeds through various stages in developing and refining his ability to represent objects and events in the world with thoughts in his mind.

In expanding Piaget's views, Jerome Bruner (132, 133) has specified three modes through which the child represents the world: the *enactive,* the *ikonic,* and the *symbolic.* The infant starts with the enactive mode, using actions to represent things and events. For example, when shown a telephone and asked what is done with it, he may make a dialing motion with his finger or put an imaginary receiver to his ear. Between eighteen and twenty-four months of age he begins using the ikonic mode, representing the world with visual images and learning to solve problems through manipulating these mental images. If the average three-year-old is asked, for instance, "which is bigger, a horse or dog?", he probably compares the two in his mind's eye before giving an answer. At around six or seven years of age, he makes a transition to the symbolic mode in his problem-solving, using language more and more in representing the world. His thinking goes beyond action and mental images to the use of symbols. He can solve an arithmetic problem, for example, without having to count objects in his head.

Through language, which involves perhaps the highest form of cognitive activity, the child attaches symbols to objects, events, and ideas to communicate with himself and others about the past, present, and future (134). His communication with himself requires the manipulation of symbols in his mind, as is done in reasoning and concept formation. His communication with others consists of two aspects: a receptive component, which allows him to interpret and comprehend symbols; and an expressive component, through which he expresses symbols intelligibly to others. As stressed earlier, the autistic child, although he may speak, is greatly impaired in both receptive and expressive language, even at the most basic gestural level. For this reason, language and other cognitive functions have assumed critical importance in the biogenic theories to be considered shortly.

These psychological functions—sensation, perception, and cognition—must be translated into observable responses in order to be studied. With refined techniques we can now measure changes in brain potential as a function of stimulus input and infer that certain sensory and perceptual processes are working, at least in the brain. However, in most research we can infer nothing about these functions without some type of motor output, whether it be speaking, pointing one's finger, shaking one's head, or winking one's eye. The child, therefore, must have certain motor capabilities that result in articulate speech or coordinated and meaningful muscle movements which reflect what psychological level he is operating on. Even a reflex, such as an eye blink to some visual stimulus coming rapidly at the eye, requires muscle action, though the whole process goes no higher than the sensory-motor level. At a higher level, a bright mute needs certain motor capabilities to communicate abstract ideas through sign language.

The functional components depicted in the diagram interact not only with the child's motor capabilities but with each other. Even if the child's cognitive ability is intact, for example, his sensory and perceptual functions also have to be working if he is to learn certain concepts. A congenitally blind child with good conceptual ability will be unable to learn the concept of "redness" since he cannot see the color and respond to it selectively in different contexts. Or a bright six-year-old with a deficit in form perception may have difficulty in learning the concept of triangularity. Defects in sensory ability may also affect response output, as in the congenitally deaf child who shows limited speech or the blind child who shows stereotypic motor behavior or "blindisms." To complicate matters even more, the motor responses in turn become stimuli for the vestibular receptors in the inner ear and proprioceptors in the muscles, tendons, and joints, thereby forming a feedback loop which allows the child to make adjustments in these responses.

Before turning to the theories that refer to these functions, we should keep in mind that the functions themselves are convenient concepts which help us in trying to understand and explain what may be going on between stimulus and response in the autistic child. We cannot, of course, directly observe his sensation, perception, or cognition but only their end products: his speech and motor behavior. From the autistic child's failure to respond with flexible, meaningful speech to our questions, we infer, for example, that there is little intervening cognition or thought on his part. From his bizarre motor behavior or "autisms" we may also infer that he is reacting to, or trying to compensate for, diminished or distorted sensations and perceptions in a manner similar to the blind child who shows "blindisms."

All of these psychological functions—the sensory, perceptual, and cognitive—can be affected by the emotional or affective responsiveness of the child, and this responsiveness is determined by both intrinsic organic variables and social experience. An intensely anxious or fearful child, for example, shows problems in attending to incoming stimuli, organizing and attaching meaning to them, and forming concepts. A great deal of the controversy about autism centers around the question of which comes first—the emotional condition or the perceptual and cognitive problems. The psychogenic theorists, as noted in the last chapter, think that the autistic child has suffered social stress or trauma that includes a severe emotional reaction; this reaction, in turn, affects perceptual and cognitive functioning that would otherwise be normal. Many of the biogenic theorists, on the other hand, think that the cognitive and perceptual defects lead to the abnormal emotional and social symptoms. Since Rimland's hypotheses clearly epitomize this latter position, the discussion starts with his theory.

Rimland's Theory of Perceptual-Cognitive Impairment

Rimland (7) proposed that the autistic child has deficits in certain basic perceptual and conceptual functions that co-exist with intact sensory functions and motor skills. The child has difficulty in organizing and attaching meaning to sensations. Though his rote memory is usually good, he cannot relate new stimuli to remembered experience; he perceives each experience as totally new, unrelated to past experiences. Auditory stimuli, as mentioned before, appear to be registered and played back to him in tape recorder fashion with little or no intervening attachment of meaning or formation of concepts. Unlike normal children, he memorizes "nonsense" material as easily as meaningful material. Moreover, his basic inability to attach meaning to experience and to form concepts interferes with his social and personality development. He is unable to perceive the significance of social attachments to people, and he is unable to develop the concept of "self" as it applies to himself or to others. These deficits in the social and personality areas, then, are secondary to the primary cognitive defect.

In discussing the possible cause of autism, Rimland noted that the autistic child, since he typically has such bright parents, is genetically predisposed toward very high intelligence. Because his nervous system is developing at a more rapid rate than the normal child, he is more vulnerable to brain damage due to certain conditions during the birth process or newborn period. Many autistic children, according to Rimland, have been administered excessive amounts of medical oxygen; their highly sensitive nervous system cannot tolerate it and brain damage may occur. This brain damage impairs the child's cognitive and perceptual functions while certain vestiges of high intelligence remain, primarily in memory and motor areas.

Rimland speculated that the site for such damage could be the reticular activating system, since it serves as an arousal and integrating system for incoming stimuli in the brain. In the normal person the reticular formation serves to "unscramble" incoming sensations and to code them by giving them meaning so that they in turn "can trigger relevant memories" in the person's mind. Rimland hypothesized that the autistic child, because of damage to this system, is incapable of attaching meaning to incoming sensations. The sensory input passes through the child's central nervous system with no interpretation and emerges relatively unchanged in his responses. For example, the speech that he hears is rotely recorded and reproduced in a literal manner rather than being understood. In terms of the diagram, the incoming stimuli go almost directly from the sensory component to response output, bypassing the perceptual and cognitive components except for memory.

In short, Rimland views the classically autistic child as having, before birth, the genetic potential for brilliance. This brilliance, though, is never fulfilled because his precociously developing, highly sensitive brain is damaged very early and is never able to integrate experiences at the higher cognitive levels. His seemingly paradoxical behavior represents his attempts to cope with his world with the lower-level skills that survived the damage.

Rimland's biogenic theory represents a major milestone in the development of scientific thinking about autism. It caused people to question the prevailing psychogenic dogma, stimulated a great deal of research, and set the stage for the development of some new perspectives on autism.

Autism as a Cognitive-Language Disorder

It begins to look, more and more disturbingly, as if the gift of language is the single human trait that marks us all genetically, setting us apart from all the rest of life. Language is, like nest-building, or hive-making, the universal and biologically specific activity of human beings. We engage in it communally, compulsively, and automatically. We cannot be human without it; if we were to be separated from it our minds would die, as surely as bees lost from the hive.

We are born knowing how to use language. The capacity to recognize syntax, to organize and deploy words into intelligible sentences, is innate in the human mind. . . . As chicks are endowed with an innate capacity to read information in the shapes of overhanging shadows, telling hawks from other birds, we can identify the meaning of grammar in a string of words, and we are born this way. . . . The universal attributes of language are genetically set; we do not learn them, or make them up as we go along. (135, pp. 89-90)

In the quotation above, taken from his book *The Lives of a Cell,* Lewis Thomas proposes two things about language. First, it is the uniquely human trait that distinguishes us from other living organisms and provides the essential substrate for our being human. Second, it is genetically programmed into the human mind with universal attributes reminiscent of those proposed by Kant. Thomas has based his conclusions on the work of the controversial linguist Noam Chomsky (136) who believes that human beings come into the world with a specific genetic ability for decoding and encoding language, for discerning and expressing meaning through speech and other modes of communication.

If we accept these propositions and apply them to the autistic child, we may theorize that his extreme difficulty in relating to people, his inability to be "human," is based on an intrinsic language deficiency. Several researchers have proposed such a theory, most notably Rutter (137), Ricks and Wing (47, 52), and Churchill (45).

In an article appearing in 1968, the British psychiatrist Michael Rutter (137) concluded that autistic children have a central disorder of language which involves both the understanding of language and the use of language or conceptual skills in thinking. He suggested that this language disorder is the primary handicap and that the other autistic symptoms are secondary. In a more recent article (56) he suggested that other cognitive abilities are also impaired, but he still indicted language as the primary handicap.

In supporting the cognitive-language disorder theory, Rutter and Bartak (56) have pointed out that retardation of speech and language is virtually ubiquitous in autism and that lack of response to sounds is often the first symptom noted. Further, use of language, along with IQ level, serves as the most reliable early predictor of later adjustment in the autistic person. These authors also have stressed that the autistic child's impairment in language differs significantly from that found in the retarded or aphasic child. The autistic child has more difficulty than the aphasic child in transferring information from one sensory modality to another, comprehending meaning of the spoken word, and using gestures. The reversal of pronouns and echolalia, which are much more common in the autistic child than in the aphasic child, also reflect basic defects in comprehension. These authors think, then, that autism represents a more severe and pervasive language handicap than that found in aphasia.

Rutter's British colleagues, L. M. Ricks and Lorna Wing, have proposed that autism is a condition which involves a number of specific impairments occurring in combination and giving rise to a recognizable set of symptoms (47). They have suggested, however, that the basic problem in autistic individuals is a "specific difficulty in handling symbols, which affects language, nonverbal communication, and many other aspects of cognitive and social activity" (p. 216).

In developing their theory that autism is a language disorder, Ricks and Wing (47) contrasted the language development of normal children with that of autistic children. The early language development of the normal child, according to the research of Ricks, is independent of social reinforcement. This early language includes the vocal signals of the infant that precede speech and convey emotional states; it also includes the first sound-labels used by the baby. As the child learns to generalize (or form concepts), he may initially apply these labels according to a classification system that differs from that used by the adults in his world. These labels may not correspond to any real word; but yet they are used by the child in a logical, consistent way. At a certain stage, for example, many normal infants use the label "Dada" for any grown male in their presence. Ricks and Wing cited the case of one normal child who applied the same sound-label to light bulb, airplane, moon, and bird (all of which are objects usually seen above).

As the normal child grows, his brain, according to these authors, is inherently organized to constantly scan, check, and look for similarities in stimuli in his world—that is, to form concepts. Further, his ability to label these concepts is an inborn function of his brain. The earliest categories are self-generated but the rules for classification are constantly being revised through the child's experience, which includes conversation and social interaction. This built-in mechanism "for scanning, classifying, and reclassifying" may be the foundation for the later ability to arrange verbal symbols according to grammatical rules, which are altered and become more complicated as the child matures.

In addition to proposing this intrinsic mechanism, necessary for early language development, Ricks and Wing used the concept of "inner language" in their theory. Inner language refers to "the store of concepts in coded (symbolic) form which grows as the child acquires competence in understanding and using language" (p. 216). The normal child draws upon this store of symbols when confronted with a new situation. He compares the new stimuli with those stored and revises old concepts or forms new ones. His formation of revised or new concepts, then, is not only a function of new experience but of his store of "inner language." Thus he builds new abstractions on the base of old ones and is limited only by his ability "to marshall and handle all the necessary coded material" (p. 217).

The autistic child, according to Ricks and Wing, appears to have some severe defect in the mechanism that underlies the normal scanning, checking, and classifying of experience. Rather than learning words through "an active processing of experience," he can only learn them passively and rotely by operant conditioning. The words in his "inner language," if he develops language at all, fail to assume the subtle overt tones and nuances of meaning that they have for the normal child. Instead, they seem to have the identical meaning they had when originally learned. Because of his good rote memory, he may be able to learn and store a great deal of verbal material, such as sayings, TV commercials, catechisms, and so on. But he does not appear "to be aware of the undertones and overtones, the many associations, some clear and obvious, others fleeting, hard to grasp, but none the less capable of evoking ideas and emotions, which give words the power and significance they have for normal people" (p. 217). As Ricks and Wing put it, "The autistic child lacks any feeling for the poetry and humor or language, even when his grasp of vocabulary and grammar is adequate" (p. 217). He cannot appreciate subtle verbal humor (as in a pun), express an impromptu, reasoned opinion on a topic, or invent an imaginary story. He also has severe problems in comprehending other people's feelings because he cannot "read" the subtle nonverbal cues, convert them to a given context, and relate them to any stored "ideas" of how people show emotions.

Through their excellent verbal memory, some autistic children can compensate for, or at least disguise, their language problems. They appear to store material and retrieve it in the automated manner of a computer. Like a computer, their operations with this material are rigidly programmed. Ricks and Wing pointed out that some can do long, numerical calculations in their heads and a few can play chess, although not creatively. But in doing these things, they follow stringent, inflexible rules that can be applied without variation. These rote memory skills can be misleading and give the impression that these children are making good progress in learning. They may be able to recite verbatim passages or facts but are at a loss to discuss the implications of such material. (One autistic boy could parrot Hamlet's soliloquy, "To be or not to be; that is the question," but could not begin to explain its meaning. Bettelheim, of course, would have a field day in explaining why the child recited this particular phrase.)

According to Ricks and Wing, the autistic child's preoccupation with repetitive activities and stimulation is related to his strengths and weaknesses—his ability to remember patterns and his inability to deal with meanings. He is attracted toward those predictable experiences that can be rotely reproduced and demand no spontaneous interpretation. So he may derive pleasure from the rhythm and the melodic pattern of a Mozart symphony, or the redundancy and symmetry of circular objects, or the interlocking structure of a jigsaw puzzle; yet he cannot enjoy or appreciate a poem, a joke, or story, or any other experience that requires drawing upon a store of associations. Even the most competent autistic adults, as noted in a later chapter, are rigid creatures of habit who live highly patterned lives and are unable to cope with unexpected events. Although they may be dependable employees, their work must be well-structured and follow a rigid set of rules. They are usually unsociable and eccentric, probably because of their inability to grasp the myriad meanings in social interaction.

Ricks and Wing think that the study of the typical language problems of autistic children helps in understanding language development in normal children. As the following passage indicates, they think that such development cannot be acceptably explained with a behavioristic or environmentalist argument.

> The characteristic problems in using language found in autistic children can throw some light on language development in normal children. In the opinion of the present authors, the purely behavioristic model does not provide a satisfactory explanation of this ability, observed in normal children, to categorize objects and events in the environment and then to enlarge and change the system of classification in the light

of new experiences. This behavior strongly suggests that the human brain actively imposes order on incoming information and is not just a passive recipient waiting to be conditioned into storing the appropriate data. (47, pp. 219-220)

Although Ricks and Wing, as well as Rutter, believe that language impairment plays a predominant role in the development of autism, they acknowledge that other cognitive and perceptual handicaps may also contribute to the basic syndrome. Don Churchill (45), who has done extensive research on the language of autistic children, has assumed a somewhat stronger stance; he has asserted that the language deficits "are the necessary and sufficient cause of those phenomena common to all autistic children, while other types of disabilities (perceptual, visual memory, etc.) might account for some of the differences among autistic children" (p. 130). In short, Churchill thinks that the common denominator in all autistic children is the language handicap. However, these theoretical differences regarding the causal significance of language in autism are related, as Churchill has pointed out, to the definition of language and cognition that the theorist adheres to.

Despite these differences, Rutter, Ricks and Wing, and Churchill agree that all autistic children show significant impairment in language from the lowest to the highest levels, from simple gestures to abstract symbols. With reference to the diagram, this defect is within the cognitive component, which includes language and the use of symbols as the highest function. If the impairment is at such a high cognitive level, we may wonder how the peculiarities of sensory and motor behavior shown by the young autistic child can be explained, especially since these deviations emerge at an earlier stage than the language problem. This raises the question that perhaps the primary impairment in autism is at a more basic level than the cognitive one.

Autism as a Perceptual-Motor or Sensorimotor Disorder

In a number of articles (e.g., 3, 8, 38, 138), Edward Ornitz and Edward Ritvo of the University of California at Los Angeles (UCLA) have proposed that the autistic child may indeed be suffering from a more basic disturbance than the cognitive one. In their earlier formulations they suggested that the basic problem is the child's inability to maintain perceptual constancy (38). The normal child, as mentioned earlier, uses perceptual constancy in perceiving objects as being the same from time to time and in tying present perceptions to past perceptions. The autistic child, according to Ornitz and Ritvo, is unable to perceive identical objects in the environment as the same each time; each time the object looks new and strange to him. The child reveals this perceptual inconstancy through his tendency to overreact or underreact to stimulus input, through his bizarre motor behavior, and through his failure to distinguish between himself and objects in environment.

In later articles these authors suggested that *sensorimotor inconstancy* may be a better label for the basic defect than perceptual inconstancy (138). The autistic child, according to this view, shows a lack of sensorimotor integration as evidenced by faulty modulation of sensory input and motor output. His failure to adequately modulate incoming sensations is reflected in his hypo- and hyper-sensitivity to different stimuli; as mentioned above, he overreacts to some and underreacts to others. His difficulty in modulating motor output is revealed in his bizarre motility patterns. These unusual motor patterns, alternate between brief states of catatonic inhibition and flurries of stereotypic movement; and they often occur when the child is in a state of general excitation brought on by internal and external sensory stimuli. The child engages in these atypical motor responses, then, because he is unable to integrate the sensory input with appropriate motor output.

To support this interpretation, Ornitz (138) cited psychological studies that demonstrate that autistic children, rather than learning primarily through their eyes and ears (distal receptors) as most children do, rely more heavily on the proximal senses; these senses include touch, kinesthesis, and the vestibular senses (balance and body position). These theorists propose, then, that the autistic child—when he spins and flicks objects, flaps and oscillates his hands and arms, whirls and rocks his body—may be trying to order a confused world through kinesthetic and vestibular feedback. He is trying, in Ornitz's words, "to make *sense* out of *sensation*" in his environment, an environment that includes his own body and its parts.

Since the earliest symptoms of autism are those of deviant responses to sensory input and deviant motility, Ornitz and Ritvo contend that this disturbance of sensorimotor integration is more basic than the cognitive problems that appear later. In terms of the diagram, then, most of the problem is in the sensory component in relation to motor output and feedback loop. Ornitz (138) hypothesized that a "dysfunction of a complex circuitry involving the central connections of the vestibular system within the cerebellum and the brain stem may be responsible for the strange sensorimotor behavior observed in autistic children" (p. 130). According to Ornitz, this proposed sensorimotor dysfunction, although it involves subcortical neural mechanisms or "lower brain" functions, may affect the way the autistic child learns about his environment and develops his body image.

Autism as an Impairment in Arousal Mechanisms

While the theorists considered so far in this chapter have differed in what they believe to be the central problem in autism, they agree that it is not an emotional or affective disturbance. The basic difficulty is an impairment in the child's ability to interpret and integrate incoming stimuli at one level or another. They also agree that it is a biogenic rather than psychogenic disorder. But we should remember that the terms "biogenic" and "emotional disturbance" are not mutually exclusive. As noted before, Kanner (1) concluded his original article by proposing that autism is an inborn, affective disturbance. Autistic children, he assumed, "come into the world with innate inability to form the usual, biologically provided affective contact with people, just as other children come into the world with innate physical or intellectual handicaps" (p. 250).

Although Kanner did not specify the mechanism underlying the proposed affective disturbance in autism, other researchers have attempted to do so. Hutt and Hutt (139, 140) of Oxford, England, have proposed that the autistic child suffers from a severe form of introversion that is organically based. The Hutts related this extreme introversion to the high degree of physiological arousal that they believe is continually present in autistic children. They based this high-arousal theory on their own research with autistic children and on findings from ethological studies which show that animals engage in "autistic" stereotypic behavior and withdrawal in states of high arousal.

Using telemetered EEG (brain-wave) recordings and behavioral observations of autistic children in familiar and unfamiliar settings, the Hutts and their associates obtained data which they interpreted as showing these children to be in a chronic state of high arousal (141). They found, too, that as the environment surrounding the children became more complex, their EEGs became more desynchronized and their stereotypic behavior more frequent. Looking at this finding from a biological perspective, they hypothesized that the autistic behaviors, such as the stereotypic movements, serve as adaptive safety devices which the child uses to minimize or prevent the unpleasant experience of excessive excitation or arousal. Since he is already in a state of high arousal, the autistic child tries to protect himself from the further arousal that is evoked by unfamiliar stimuli or social situations. For example, his gaze-aversion is an attempt to avoid the intense level of arousal associated with looking directly in the eyes of another person.

The Hutts suggested that this continually high physiological arousal may be due to a defect in the nonascending reticular system, which serves as the "arousal" center in the brain. Because of this postulated defect, the arousal system in the autistic child is chronically activated and operating continually at an abnormally high level.

One shortcoming of the Hutts's arousal theory is that it fails to explain adequately the finding that many autistic children appear to be in a state of low arousal rather than high arousal. DesLauriers and Carlson (142) have tried to reconcile these conflicting findings by theorizing that some autistic children are in a state of chronically high arousal while others are in a state of chronically low arousal.

In their book *Your Child Is Asleep* (142) these authors proposed that autism is an extreme developmental deviation that is present from birth. The autistic child suffers from severe sensory and emotional deprivation which results from an internal barrier within the child, a barrier that shuts out normal sensory and affective experience. Their theory is based on a proposal by Routtenberg (143) which states that there is a reciprocal relationship between two systems within the brain—the ascending reticular activating system and the limbic system. The first is thought to be an activating and energizing system while the second controls reward and affective stimulation such as pleasure and pain. In the normal person these two systems are in a state of balance, with each inhibiting the activity of the other.

DesLauriers and Carlson postulated that in the autistic child the two systems are out of balance, failing to reciprocally suppress each other. The imbalance, depending on its direction, can result in either a *hypoactive* autistic child, described as being a "good," quiet undemanding baby, or a *hyperactive* autistic child, described as being an irritable and hypersensitive baby. Because of the differences in the direction of the imbalance, the hypoactive child receives minimal stimulus input whereas the hyperactive child is bombarded with intensely high stimulation. Nevertheless, both types of children are suffering from sensory deprivation since neither receives stimulation that has meaning.

Since this theory proposes abnormal functioning of the limbic system, which plays a basic role in emotional functioning and experiences of pleasure and reward, the affective impairment in autism is accounted for. If this system is continually suppressed, then the child does not experience normal reward and has difficulty in forming appropriate affective association. There is, in effect, an innate affective barrier which prevents the child from forming emotional attachments and experiencing the positive reinforcement necessary for learning. A later chapter considers the treatment technique that DesLauriers and Carlson have used in trying to break down this barrier.

So discussion of the theories regarding the basic problems and underlying causes of autism ends here. Many more pages could have been devoted to other theories that deal with these issues—theories that are variations on the basic themes presented in this chapter and the preceding one. The number and diversity of these theories attest to the broad heuristic impact that this relatively rare disorder has had on scientific thinking about psychological development and the variables that determine it. I have stressed those theories that bring into clear focus the controversial issues of what autism basically is and how it is caused.

The final resolution of these issues will come, of course, when the cause (or causes) of autism is determined. Only then can clear steps toward prevention of autism be taken. Until then we can evaluate the theories on how well they help us in explaining and tying together the existing facts about autism. The evidence that bears upon our evaluation of these theoretical issues, particularly the psychogenic versus biogenic proposals, are now considered.

9 Inferences and Insights

Although there are many theories on the cause of autism, the cause is still unknown. We do, however, have access to an accumulating body of evidence that relates to the general issue of psychogenesis versus biogenesis and provides insights into possible underlying causes. This evidence is important for theoretical and scientific reasons, for it helps us to evaluate and refine theories and formulate hypotheses for further research that may lead to causes. It is important, too, for practical and personal reasons; it should provide the basis for development of more realistic attitudes in professionals who work with autistic children and their parents and should alleviate the unwarranted guilt that the parents may experience.

Evidence Against Parental Causation

The advocates of the psychogenic view of autism, such as Bettelheim, have argued that the basic cause of autism lurks somewhere in the family atmosphere—in the parents' personality and child-rearing attitudes and practices. They have stressed the causal significance of the "classic" parental picture reported in the early studies by Kanner and Eisenberg, who described the parents as emotional refrigerators, cold, aloof, intellectual, and reserved in their relationship with their children. The parents, according to this view, are largely responsible for the development of autism. After taking a careful look at the recent findings on parental and family characteristics, however, we can find little support for this position.

As noted in the chapter on parents and family, more and more research indicates that the "classic" parental personality is likely an artifact of the early studies. In their review of research on family factors in autism, McAdoo and DeMyer (111) concluded that parents of autistic children generally fail to show "extreme personality traits such as coldness, obsessiveness, social anxiety, or extreme rage" (p. 165). Nor do they exhibit any deficiencies in "acceptance, nurturing, warmth, feeding, and tactile and general stimulation of their infants" (p. 165). Further, these parents show no more signs of emotional problems than parents of children with nonpsychotic organic or emotional disorders. These authors stated, too, that research findings support the conclusion that the confusion and uncertainty shown by most parents of autistic children, rather than playing a causal role, is more the consequence of the continued stress of trying to understand and rear an autistic child.

In her assessment of research on parental personality and child-rearing techniques related to autism, Lorna Wing (112) reached essentially the same conclusions. "The evidence," she concluded, "for theories which consider parental abnormalities to be the primary cause of childhood autism is unconvincing" (p. 74). Further, she could find no evidence to support the assumption that the parents are deviant in their child-rearing techniques or that parental psychopathology exacerbates or precipitates the autistic disturbance in a "vulnerable" child.

Even if there were a "classic" parental personality picture associated with autism, it would be difficult to attribute a causal role to it. Rimland (7), for example, accepted the "classic" parental personality as fact but presented a convincing case for genetic rather than environmental causation. In his carefully considered argument for biogenesis, he also pointed out that most parents in the general population who do fit the "classic" personality picture do not have autistic children. If the parental personality is the critical causal factor, then the incidence of autism should be much higher than it is. Every day we see compulsive, reserved, intellectual parents who, according to some psychogenic theorists, should have autistic children. Their children, however, are almost always normal.

Think of the many parents we have seen who are under intense, sustained psychological and physical stress—parents without jobs, or with highly stressful jobs, parents with chronic, incurable diseases, parents struggling to survive against all sorts of odds. This stress, according to Tinbergen's psychogenic position, would be transmitted to their infants or young children who in turn would develop autism. This rarely occurs.

We even see parents who willfully subject their children to physical and psychological abuse and neglect of the most flagrant kind. If any children would resort to the extreme withdrawal that is presumed to occur in autism, it seems that these children would. Even the "battered child," broken and bruised by his parents, usually bounces back with a social resilience that is difficult to explain. Instead of withdrawing, he still shows an emotional attachment to his parents and usually reaches out urgently for acceptance and positive attention (144, 145). With all his physical and emotional scars, he does not develop autism.

Another fact that is difficult to reconcile with the psychogenic view is the consistent finding that most siblings of autistic children, except in cases of identical twins, are normal. For example, the first 100 autistic children seen by Kanner had 131 brothers and sisters; of this group of siblings, 117 were considered to be normal in emotional development (106). These siblings were probably scrutinized much more closely for problems than siblings of children with other disorders. Other research has confirmed this finding (5, 7, 58, 146). In reviewing the sibling studies, Rimland (7) cited the case of a family having one autistic child in the middle of a series of eleven normal children.

These studies on siblings cast serious doubt on the hypothesis that the parents are causal agents for autism. Surely parents pathogenic enough to engender such a profound disturbance as autism should have at least some deleterious effect on the emotional development of their other children.

Another fact that does not fit the psychogenic theory is that autistic children are found in families from various cultures throughout the world, cultures that differ widely in family structure and child-rearing practices (6, 8). Despite these differences, the behavior of the autistic child from a small town in Mississippi is strikingly similar to that of the autistic child from Tokyo. These highly specific behavior patterns appear, then, to be relatively independent of cultural milieu.

These findings as a whole reveal no consistent relationships between parental, family, and cultural characteristics and the presence of an autistic child. Hence, they provide no support for the notion that autism is caused by, or even correlated with, factors in the psychological environment. In Chapter 6 it was noted, however, that many studies have reported a disproportionate number of autistic children from families of higher socioeconomic and intellectual levels (111); but research that controls for selection bias, such as the recent study by Schopler, Andrews, and Strupp (110), may eventually prove this to be a spurious finding. Assuming, though, that the finding is valid, it offers no strength to the psychogenic position. As Wing (112) has stated, "Intelligence and higher social class are usually considered to be an advantage in coping with life rather than the reverse" (p. 74), and these qualities typically are not associated with poor child-rearing practices.

On the basis of all of the evidence on family characteristics, then, it is difficult to develop a psychogenic argument that holds water. On the other hand, there are several lines of evidence that support the biogenic hypothesis of an organic basis for autism.

Evidence for Genetic Components

In looking for possible causes for autism, it makes sense to start with genes and chromosomes. The fact that autism appears to be present from birth or discernible at a very young age suggests a genetic component to the disorder (1, 7). Rather than being normal up to a certain age and then withdrawing from social interaction, the autistic child in most cases never forms social relationships in the first place. He appears to enter the world with a deficit in responsiveness to certain stimuli, especially social stimuli.

Even in those children whose autistic symptoms reportedly appear after the first or second year, genetic factors may still be operating. We are just beginning to discover how intellectual and behavioral development can sometimes be profoundly influenced by genes—minute agents whose effects are sometimes immediate and sometimes delayed but nonetheless significant.

In genetic disorders the symptoms may appear at various stages of development, the timing varying from one disease to another but often precisely programmed within a given disorder. In Down's Syndrome, for example, the physical stigmata are present in the newborn and the retarded development apparent soon afterward. These children typically exhibit a progressive deceleration in the rate of intellectual development as they move from early childhood to adolescence (147). Their genetically determined cognitive impairment becomes more prominent, then, in late childhood and then levels off. In Tay-Sachs disease, a progressive neurological illness largely confined to Jewish babies with ancestors from eastern Europe, the genetic programming is quicker and far more devastating. The infant is socially alert and develops normally for the first six months or so; he achieves head control and often sits up but then loses these skills, showing rapid, progressive mental and motor deterioration and usually dying before three or four years of age (148).

While genes can show their effects with tragic swiftness in diseases such as Tay-Sachs, they can delay their influences for years in other disorders. In Huntington's chorea, the person is normal until thirty-five or so; then he begins to exhibit involuntary movements of the limbs and progressive mental deterioration (149). The folksinger Woodie Guthrie, although afflicted with this disease, led an active and productive life for almost forty years until the genes began to exert their grim influence.

With the three disorders just described the genetic culprit, despite differences in its time of expression, can be clearly indicted. In Down's Syndrome, it is an extra chromosome; in Tay-Sachs disease, a recessive gene; in Huntington's chorea, a dominant gene. While no specific genetic agent of this type has been found in autism, the available evidence from studies of identical twins supports the hypothesis that there is at least a genetic predisposition toward the disorder (7, 111, 150).

Identical twins, of course, have identical sets of genes, while fraternal twins or other siblings do not. Most research indicates a high concordance rate for autism in identical twins; that is, when one identical twin suffers from autism, his counterpart is likely also to have the disorder (3, 7, 8, 151). Fraternal twins, however, show an extremely low concordance rate for autism, although both are born at the same time and likely are exposed to highly similar environments in terms of family stress and parental personalities and attitudes. As noted earlier, other siblings are almost never autistic. We may infer from these findings, then, that genes play a more influential role in the development of autism than the psychosocial atmosphere of the family.

The specific role that genetic influences take in autism is not clear although some hunches can be drawn from research findings. In her review of evidence relating to this question, Anne Spence (150) of UCLA concluded that autism could not be due to an aberration of the chromosomes (as in Down Syndrome) or a single gene (as in Tay-Sachs disease) but rather to polygenic effects, that is, the cumulative, interactive effects of a number of genes. She proposed that certain aspects of autism may be inherited while others are not. In support of this proposal, the results of some studies (e.g., 151) suggest that the genetic component may be the cognitive-language disability, which some researchers (e.g., 45) think is the primary impairment common to all autistic children.

Autism and Brain Damage

Although certain components of autism may have some genetic basis, other influences probably have to be operating in order for the child to show the fullblown syndrome. The influences may occur prenatally, perinatally, or postnatally, but they seem to have the common result of brain damage or dysfunction. A substantial amount of evidence indicates that autistic symptoms are associated with neurological dysfunction or conditions attributable to brain damage.

Autism, as was noted earlier, occurs about three or four times more frequently in males than in females; this male-female ratio is the same as that found in disorders associated with neurological damage or dysfunction (7). Further, recent studies have reported more signs of neurological dysfunction in autistic children than were noted in earler studies; in fact, these dysfunctions become more apparent as the children grow older, even in those children who originally showed no such problems (59, 73, 152). For example, the percent of these children who have abnormal EEGs ("brain-wave" recordings) is significantly higher than once suspected. As they grow older and enter adolescence and adulthood, about one-fourth or more of these children develop convulsive or seizure disorders (73). Even though most autistic children exhibit no gross neurological problems, many may show one or more so-called "soft" neurological signs such as incoordination, reflex anomalies, strabismus ("cross-eye"), or poor muscle tone (3).

A number of studies have reported a high incidence of autistic behavior in children suffering from conditions that are clearly the consequence of brain damage. Infantile spasms and early brain infections such as meningitis and encephalitis are often followed by either partial or complete autism (81). Many children with phenylketonuria also show a high incidence of autistic symptoms. Phenylketonuria, or PKU, is a genetic disorder of metabolism which, if undetected and untreated during the first few months of life, causes brain damage and severe mental retardation. Many children with PKU were diagnosed at one time as autistic. Consider the following excerpt from Donald Cohen's testimony regarding autism before the United States House of Representatives:

> Several weeks ago I saw a preschool aged girl with all of the classical signs of childhood autism: social aloofness, developmental retardation, stereotypic behavior, emotional lability, and disturbed language functioning. Metabolic evaluation, however, revealed that the youngster was suffering from an entity for which practically every child in the United States is screened during the first week of life, phenylketonuria.
>
> Before the time of mass screening for PKU, many children with this inborn disease of metabolism were diagnosed as having childhood autism, a diagnosis which was often supported with the observation that many of these children were attractive, agile-appearing, blond haired, blue-eyed youngsters with no obvious signs of brain malformation. The autistic syndrome can be found associated with other organic disturbances, including such dysfunctions as lead intoxication and encephalitis; other disorders of amino acid metabolism such as PKU; retrolental fibroplasia and other conditions which lead to blindness (153, p. 10).

Prevention of the mental retardation associated with PKU is a remarkable scientific achievement with profound implications. Those children who would have been serverely retarded with measured IQs of thirty-five or lower are now developing normally with IQs of 100 or higher, all because their biochemical anomaly was detected at birth and a special diet implemented to avert brain damage (154). The autistic behavior that they might have shown was also prevented. The same applies to children who have avoided rubella syndrome through the vaccine.

Autism and Rubella Syndrome

If a pregnant woman contracts rubella (German measles) during the first three months of her pregnancy, the chances are quite high that the child she is carrying will also be infected. This infection may produce a variety of congenital defects that are evident when the child is born. These include cataracts, heart defects, deafness, and neurological impairment. Fortunately, with the widespread use of the rubella vaccine, congenital rubella is now relatively rare in newborn babies. This was not the case, however, in the mid-1960s, when an estimated twenty thousand to thirty thousand infants were born with congenital defects due to the rubella epidemic that swept the United States in 1964. These children have been the subject of many studies, such as those conducted by Stella Chess of New York University Medical Center (96, 155).

Chess was primarily interested in determining the psychological consequences of congenital rubella. In the first study (96) she assessed the behavior of 243 children with this syndrome and concluded that the incidence of behavioral disturbances in these youngsters was much higher than in the general population. She was especially struck with the high frequency of autism in the group. She identified ten children as classically autistic and eight more as having a significant number of autistic features. These figures, of course, are much higher than the expectancy rate of one to five autistic children per ten thousand in the general population.

Chess interpreted these results as lending strong support to the theory of organic causation in autism. She found no evidence, on the other hand, to support the psychogenic hypothesis; the parents represented diverse socioeconomic levels and failed to fit the "refrigerator" stereotype. The common element in the history of these children was not a rejecting mother but rather a rubella virus that had invaded their rapidly developing nervous system during the prenatal period. Chess concluded therefore that the common denominator in these autistic children might be brain damage.

There is an interesting sequel to this story. Chess (155) did a follow-up study on these children when they were eight to nine years of age. She was especially concerned with seeing if any changes had occurred in those eighteen children originally diagnosed as having partial or complete autism. Of the ten children who earlier had shown complete autism, three had recovered, a finding that is inconsistent with recovery rates reported in other studies; one was considered improved and six unimproved in autistic behavior. Of the eight children who previously showed partial autism, three were recovered, four were worse, and one was not included in the follow-up study because her parents refused to bring her in. A further and unexpected finding was that four children who were not autistic before were now autistic.

Chess concluded that the best explanation for the course of the autistic symptoms and the change in clinical picture, both positive and negative, is in terms of the viral infection of the central nervous system. The course of symptoms, according to her interpretation, "has been that of a chronic infection in which recovery, chronicity, improvement, worsening, and delayed effects can all occur" (p. 80). She could find nothing to support any other interpretation.

In supporting this explanation, Chess reviewed the history of the girl who had recovered completely from the autism. At the time of follow-up the girl (who was deaf and also blind in one eye due to a cataract) was alert, cooperative, and responsive to the examiner; she showed appropriate play and social interaction. She was functioning at an average intellectual level, and her expressive and receptive language skills were good, considering her deafness. Chess pointed out that this girl's dramatic recovery took place despite a seriously traumatic family situation. Her mother had just died of cancer after a lengthy illness requiring several hospitalizations; the death took place at home and was witnessed by the girl. Her father was an alcoholic who created a home environment which prompted neighbors to request the Child Abuse Agency to take the child from the home and place her in a residential school for the deaf. The only stable influence in the immediate family was the girl's normal sister, who was two years older. Chess concluded that "under these adverse environmental circumstances, and with the continuing presence of both cataract and deafness, it would be indeed difficult to explain this child's recovery as due to any psychological cause" (p. 80).

Chess emphasized that she was not proposing that all cases of autism are caused by a viral infection of the brain; on the contrary, the most reasonable hypothesis is that autism may be the "final behavioral consequence of many different causes." However, it is of significant theoretical import, she noted, to discover that the severe, complex psychopathology that constitutes autism may be the result of a virus that invades the central nervous system—a virus whose behavioral effects are sometimes delayed.

Autism and Heller's Disease

Another organic condition that has been related to autism is Heller's disease (7, 30). This rare and controversial illness was reported first in 1908 by the Viennese educator Heller. He described a group of children who appeared to be quite normal until three or four years of age, at which time they regressed markedly in their behavioral and mental development. Although they had shown no previous emotional problems, they abruptly became fretful, negativistic, and anxious. They began to destroy toys that they had liked and played with normally before. They regressed in mental development and gradually lost the speech that previously had been normal. They continued to deteriorate in intellectual and emotional development, and none showed improvement over the years, with some dying at a very early age (156).

Despite the difference in the course and outcome of the two conditions, Heller's disease and autism show some similarities. As in classic autism, these children maintained an intelligent facial expression and intact motor functions despite their severe emotional and intellectual deterioration, and they engaged in stereotypic motor behavior. Further, these children showed no outward signs typically associated with a distinct neurological disorder or a progressive neurological disease. In fact, they were originally thought to have functional psychoses. But subsequent autopsies done on some children who were diagnosed as having Heller's disease showed diffuse degeneration of the brain, in some cases like that found in Tay-Sachs disease (30, 157).

Some researchers think that Heller's disease does not represent a distinct disease entity in itself since the underlying brain pathology overlaps with that of several other degenerative brain diseases of childhood. Others want to lump it indiscriminately into a catch-all category called "atypical development of childhood" (158). Some think however, that it does constitute a separate syndrome whose diagnostic integrity should be preserved. Regardless of this diagnostic controversy, the fact still remains that the children who were later shown to have diffuse brain damage were originally believed to be neurologically normal and suffering from a severe emotional disorder with some autistic features. It seems reasonable to assume that the autistic features were associated with the underlying brain disease, since the children were normal in emotional development before its onset.

Other Evidence for Organic Causation

In a recent review of basic research on autism, L. R. Piggott (159) of the Lafayette Clinic in Detroit considered evidence derived from a number of diverse studies and concluded that autism is associated with, and perhaps caused by, certain organic problems. In reaching this conclusion, he covered a wide range of research dealing with physical, neurophysiological, and biochemical correlates of autism; but this discussion is restricted to two recent findings that are especially noteworthy.

One finding is based upon the use of a refined technique for brain study called the pneumoencephalograph. Using this technique to examine the brains of sixteen autistic children, Hauser, DeLong, and Rosman (160) at Massachusetts General Hospital in Boston discovered abnormalities of the temporal horn in fifteen of the children. The significance of this finding is that temporal lobe structures are necessary for normal behavior in affective, social, and motivational spheres, areas in which the autistic child is greatly deficient. Temporal lobe damage is found in adult patients with Korsakoff's psychosis, a severe disturbance resulting from lengthy alcoholism, and Kluver-Bucy syndrome, a disorder in which the patient shows the "autistic" symptoms of social isolation, failure to recognize the significance of people, random repetitive hyperactivity, and bizarre, noncommunicative language. These researchers pointed out that the involved brain area in these autistic children is known to be especially vulnerable to damage from lack of oxygen (hypoxia). There was evidence for prenatal brain insult in five of the children, five had a history of seizures, and twelve had abnormal EEGs. The results, then, support the conclusion that autistic behavior may be associated with temporal lobe damage, damage that may arise from hypoxia or other conditions adversely affecting the developing brain.

Another study particularly relevant to the issue of biogenesis dealt with autopsies of autistic children. Such autopsies are quite infrequent because autistic children are typically healthy and reports of death are extremely rare. In an article published in 1976, J. K. Darby (161) reviewed all reported cases of autistic and psychotic children who had died and undergone autopsies. Out of the total of thirty-three such cases found, the autopsy revealed neuropathology in twenty-seven cases. These results speak for themselves.

Evidence Relating to the Basic Impairment

The last chapter presented theories which proposed that autism is an organically based disorder involving impairment in sensorimotor, perceptual, cognitive, or affective functions. The particular function or combination of functions involved varies from one theory to the next. Most of the well-controlled research suggests that different sensorimotor, perceptual, and cognitive functions may be impaired, although the basic or pivotal impairment remains to be determined.

Several theorists, such as Goldfarb (162) and Ornitz and Ritvo, whose theory was examined in the last chapter, have postulated that the basic impairment in autistic children is in the self-monitoring or feed-back systems, particularly the vestibular system. In a series of studies reviewed by Ornitz and Ritvo (3, 8, 138), some evidence implicating a vestibular disturbance in the brain stem has been found. If the vestibular disturbance is the basic impairment, however, it would have to have pervasive effects to account for the diverse combination of defects shown in the autistic child.

More and more research, such as that reported by Hermelin and O'Connor (50), Rutter and Bartak (56, 163), Churchill (45), and others, points to a combination of perceptual and cognitive defects that affect the development of concepts and language. These defects may prevent the autistic child from selecting, interpreting, and attaching meaning to incoming stimuli, including social stimuli. This does not mean that there are no emotional components to his disorder; it means that the basic defects prevent or hinder his development of appropriate affective attachments and emotional responsiveness to other people. His disturbed social and motor responses, then, may be secondary reactions to this basic defect in integrating and "making sense" of sensations. Just as the blind child develops compensatory mannerisms that appear strange to the sighted person, the autistic child develops seemingly bizarre behavior perhaps in an attempt to compensate for his inability to understand and cope with the world.

The research on response of autistic children to treatment and educational programs which is considered in the next section further supports the theory that many have a basic cognitive deficit. Even when many of the autistic symptoms are greatly improved, a cognitive defect remains in most of these children. They can be taught eye contact, body contact, and other forms of social responsiveness more readily than meanings, concepts, and the flexible use of language. In fact, the degree of their early cognitive and language defects, as noted previously, appears to be the best predictor of later adjustment.

Conclusions Regarding Causation

The diversity, complexity, and sheer quantity of research on autism would probably intimidate even the most eager student of the subject. The studies range from the molecular to the molar, from the bio-chemical to the behavioral. A thorough interpretation of this research exceeds the purview of this book. Despite the massive search for a cause, no clear cause has been determined. Nevertheless, the ines-capable inference drawn from the evidence reviewed in this chapter is that autism is more related to biogenic than psychogenic influences. But, to use an Oscar Wilde phrase, "the truth is rarely pure and never simple." If and when the "truth" is know about autism, this probably will be the case.

The available evidence suggests an underlying organic defect (or combination of defects) that may be associated with a combination of interacting causes, including prenatal, perinatal, and postnatal in-fluences. We could hypothesize that the same underlying damage or defect could be caused by different agents and manifested to different degrees in the combination of autistic symptoms. The classically au-tistic children, for example, who show the highest peaks of isolated ability may be those genetically predisposed to high intelligence and suffering from some subtle perinatal or postnatal trauma to the brain. Other children may show many of the same autistic symptoms with underlying brain damage resulting from untreated PKU or from pre-natal exposure to the rubella virus. It is possible, too, that the un-derlying defect or damage in some cases may impinge on brain sites controlling emotional or affective responsiveness. The main point to be drawn from this chapter is that the basic defects—whether primarily cognitive or affective or a mixture of both—appear to be more consistently associated with biological than with social factors.

If we accept the conclusion that the autistic child has a biogenic disorder, we do not deny that the disorder can be aggravated or improved by social and psychological influences. We are only rejecting the notion that the disorder is engendered by such influences, namely, parental attitudes and child-rearing techniques. It seems clear that the child-rearing methods used successfully by mothers in rearing most other children fail to work with the autistic child. The mother may naturally become quite frustrated and disappointed in her futile attempts to establish a relationship with the child. The next section explains some of the more recent treatment approaches which, rather than indicting the mother and removing the child from her care, help the mother to learn special techniques for reaching the child and making him more responsive to her and other people.

III Treatment, Outcome and Conclusions

Introduction

> You see, you start pretty much from scratch when you work with an autistic child. You have a person in the physical sense—they have hair, a nose and a mouth—but they are not people in the psychological sense. One way to look at the job of helping autistic kids is to see it as a matter of constructing a person. You have the raw materials, but you have to build the person. (164, p. 76)

The words of Ivar Lovaas of UCLA communicate the formidable challenge that the autistic child presents to the therapist. In children with other behavior disorders the therapist finds some degree of "personhood" or interpersonal responsiveness that serves as a starting point for treatment. This responsiveness may be diminished, distorted, or exaggerated, but at least it is there to work with. With most autistic children, it is not there and has not been there. You have to start with the basic elements of human responsiveness and try to gradually incorporate those into the child's behavior repertoire. As Lovaas says, "you have to build the person."

Part III considers some of the different approaches used in attempting to "build the person" of the autistic child and the related topic of what happens to him as he grows older. Despite the claims of the more ardent practitioners of different therapies, there appears to be no "cure" for autism—at least no cure related to any one approach

116

to treatment. As discussed in Chapter 13, those few autistic individuals who have "recovered" and adjusted to society as adults have done so independent of any traditional form of treatment. However, the long-range follow-up studies were necessarily conducted on persons who had reached adulthood before the advent of many of the special treatment programs developed specifically for autistic children.

In psychotherapy, whether with autistic children or persons with other types of problems, there are two opposing philosophies which govern the approach the therapist takes in treating the problem. One school of thought is generally called "psychodynamic" and is best illustrated in psychoanalytic techniques; the other is "behavioristic" and is represented in treatment using principles of learning and conditioning.

The psychodynamic therapists insist that before we can effectively treat any disorder with a presumed psychological origin, we must first formulate the "underlying cause" or "dynamics" that give rise to the disturbed behavior seen on the surface. Our treatment, then, should be directed toward remedying the inner problem or rearranging the internal dynamics of the psyche, which in turn would lead to a change in the outward behavior. In short, we should treat the cause rather than symptoms, for if we failed to get at the cause or "root of the problem," the symptoms would keep on reappearing in one form or another. The psychodynamic therapists call this reappearance of symptoms "symptom substitution."

This argument for treating the underlying cause seems at first glance to make sense, and there is little doubt that it holds for diseases for which there is an underlying physical cause that can be physically treated (for example, PKU). Problems arise, however, when we automatically apply the same argument to psychological treatment of behavioral or emotional disorders with presumed psychosocial causes. Further, the argument may not even hold for treatment of such disorders with known psychosocial causes.

The therapists from the other camp, the behaviorists, argue that we do not necessarily have to know the cause of the disorder to be able to correct or change the abnormal behavior patterns. As long as the problem behavior or emotional reactions can be eliminated, or at least improved, through application of learning principles, then why worry about the presumed cause? The psychodynamic therapist counters by saying that such superficial treatment inevitably results in the emergence of symptoms in another form. The behavior therapist then replies, "Baloney. I can show you that your symptom substitution doesn't occur."

The behavior therapist may use treatment of enuresis (bedwetting) as an example. In treating the child with this problem, he would not waste time trying to determine the underlying cause of the bedwetting or tracing it back to its origin. Using learning principles and perhaps a conditioning apparatus, he would try to teach the child to awaken and go to the bathroom rather than wetting the bed. If the child learns to do this most of the time, then the behavior therapist would consider the problem cured or at least greatly improved. Further, the behavior therapist could show that there is no symptom substitution, but rather a general improvement in other areas because of the child's improved self-image over not wetting his bed.

Although autism is far more severe and complicated than enuresis, the behavior therapists maintain that you do not need to know the cause in order to bring about improvement in the disorder with behavioral techniques. Even Bernard Rimland (125, 165), who thinks that the basic cause may be biological and ultimately treated by biochemical means, advocates the use of operant conditioning as the most effective approach at the present time.

The first two chapters of Part III contrast these two divergent approaches to treatment of the autistic child. Chapter 10 describes treatment techniques that address autism as basically an emotional or affective disorder caused either by experiences during infancy or an innate defect. Chapter 11, on the other hand, presents behavioral methods of treatment and considers some of the ethical issues raised by these methods. Chapter 12 reviews some other approaches to helping the autistic child and his parents, stressing new perspectives on treatment and education. Chapter 13 looks at what happens to autistic individuals as adolescents and adults, including the original group seen by Kanner in 1943; the early childhood signs that are related to later adjustment are also noted.

So in Part III the focus shifts from theoretical issues to more practical concerns, from the controversy over the basic nature and cause of autism to questions regarding treatment, education, and life adjustment. In spite of the change in focus, we shall see that the theoretical and practical are inseparable in our pursuit of a better understanding of autism, for in assessing the autistic child's response to treatment and education, in evaluating his long-range capability for adapting to the demands of life, we can begin to see more clearly what his basic problems may be.

10 Treatment at the Emotional Level

This chapter first examines two techniques aimed at correcting presumed underlying problems that can be traced to social interaction in infancy. Both techniques are based on the assumption that the autistic child is suffering from a severe emotional or affective disorder—a disorder precipitated at least partially by the actions and attitudes of the mother. While both approaches share the hypothesis that autism is an affective disturbance, they differ radically in their theoretical roots and actual methods of intervention with the child. After considering these two techniques, we will look briefly at the treatment devised by DesLauriers and Carlson, who also feel that autism is an affective disorder, but one that the child enters the world with.

Bettelheim's Treatment: Finding the Self

The treatment program that clearly exemplifies the traditional "psychodynamic" approach, stemming from the theory and techniques of psychoanalysis, is that used by Bruno Bettelheim of the Orthogenic School in Chicago. As noted in Chapter 7, Bettelheim (104) believes that the autistic infant is "dehumanized" by the unconscious or conscious wish of his mother that he not exist and be a part of his human family. The child therefore fails to develop a "self" or "ego" and erects defenses against the hostile world of interpersonal relations. Bettelheim's therapy, then, is directed toward "humanizing" the child through giving him a self or ego that is capable of freedom and autonomy.

The first step in Bettelheim's therapy program is to remove the child from the family environment that presumably precipitated the autistic disorder. To help the autonomous self or ego emerge, the child is then permitted to express freely his *oral, anal,* or *genital* impulses. The psychoanalytic therapist interprets the child's activity with reference to Freud's theory of psychosexual development, which postulates that the child must progress through the oral, anal, and genital stages in order to develop a normal ego or self. Since the autistic child, according to this view, has been traumatized at the most primitive level, he has to work gradually through each stage in an unrestricted atmosphere. Through such free expression the child begins to learn that all autonomy has not been denied him, and he starts to develop an independent self. For example, if he defecates on the floor and smears his feces, he is allowed to continue such activity since it serves as unthwarted expression of his autonomy. Through the gradual development of such independence over several years, most "clearly autistic" children, according to Bettelheim, can be returned to society.

In his book *The Empty Fortress,* Bettelheim presented the case histories of three "autistic" children treated at the Orthogenic School—Laurie, Marcia, and Joey, the subject of Bettelheim's widely read article, "Joey: A Mechanical Boy," in *Scientific American* (166). The case of Laurie is now briefly reviewed to illustrate Bettelheim's approach to treatment.

Laurie entered the Orthogenic School at seven years of age. She was extremely emaciated from anorexia, but pretty and well-groomed. She had not spoken for over four years. Although she had started talking at fifteen months of age, she had never addressed anyone by name or used the words "mommy" or "daddy." She began regressing at about two and one-half years of age when her young nursemaid, who had cared for her since birth, left suddenly. Laurie stopped using the few words in her vocabulary, instead making strange clucking sounds. When spanked by her mother for making these noises, Laurie quit speaking altogether. Soon afterward she gave up bowel control and withdrew into a state of almost total inertness. She would remain wherever she was put, whether on a chair, on the floor, or on the toilet, until bodily removed to another place. If she engaged in any activity, it was either ritualistic or destructive. At times she would mechanically turn magazine pages without looking at them or would tear the pages into tiny pieces. She would occasionally go into spontaneous fits of destructive activity, ripping buttons off her clothes, tearing her sheets, peeling wallpaper off the walls. When spoken to, she turned her face away. Eventually she stopped eating by herself and had to be spoon-fed.

During the first days at the Orthogenic School, Laurie refused to eat and drink, vomiting frequently and becoming more emaciated and dehydrated. She then began to eat bits of food that she could swallow without chewing, such as tiny pieces of cookie or candy. She appeared to be oblivious to her body functions, showing no expression, for example, when she defecated in her pants. Sometimes the staff did not know she had had a bowel movement until the stool had fallen from her underpants.

Within the context of the freedom of expression allowed in the Orthogenic School, Laurie gradually advanced through stages of increasing awareness of her eliminative activities. First, she began to wiggle in trying to get the stools to fall from her pants; then she started taking the feces out in her hand, playing with them as she did with her blocks; finally, she showed an awareness during the bowel movement, her face and body straining. This progression, according to Bettelheim, reflected her growing awareness of bodily functions and beginning sense of selfhood: "Having to fathom, at the late age of eight, the difference between self and nonself in the context of stools leaving her body was a fearful task. That was why Laurie now studied and restudied how her bowel movements left her body, and again and again played it all out with blocks" (p. 113). Laurie then reached the stage where she went to the toilet on her own and defecated in the commode.

After showing improvement in eliminative functions and other areas, Laurie had a severe relapse marked by a dramatic withdrawal into an infantile state—a state in which she even kept her eyes shut. Her favorite counselor had to care for her continuously as she would an infant. Then one day, while being rolled in a buggy, Laurie opened her eyes again, blinking them "open and shut as a baby might on awakening." She then appeared to start a new life. In Bettelheim's words, "From now she did original things that expressed what she wished to be dealing with. No part of it was just a taking or copying of what we offered. It was autonomous new invention; her own way, not ours, of struggling to become a person" (p. 135).

Bettelheim reported that as Laurie began to move out of her autism, her parents withdrew her from the school. Soon after that time, she was committed to a state hospital for mentally defective children, where, according to Bettelheim, she regressed to the severely autistic state that she was in when she entered the Orthogenic School.

We can gather from the case of Laurie that Bettelheim's approach is based on the assumption that the autistic child will gradually discover himself (in the most literal sense) through doing his own thing in a free, acceptant environment, even if his "thing" takes the form of refusing to feed himself, urinating on the floor, playing with feces, or masturbating openly. Imposing rules or setting limits deprives the child of his freedom to develop an autonomous ego through working through these oral, anal, and genital activities. The treatment also presumes that the autistic child has the power within himself to develop, with little direction from the therapist, this sense of selfhood which leads to appropriate socialization. The therapist, then, assumes a passive role in trying to influence the child's actions and an active role in trying to fit these actions into the psychoanalytic framework. As with most psychoanalytic therapy, it is an engrossing and fulfilling intellectual exercise for the therapist, since every action can be neatly explained and the theory confirmed. Whether or not such therapy is beneficial to most autistic children is another question.

Laurie represents an unsuccessful case, Bettelheim implied, because she left his program too soon. Bettelheim claimed, as was mentioned before, that the majority of "clearly autistic children" with whom he had worked for several years "were returned to society."

In view of the discouraging results of most follow-up studies of autistic children, his reported success is difficult to accept without qualifications. Perhaps he has been working with a select sample of autistic children—children who show the most potential for improvement in the first place or children who do not fit the classic criteria for infantile autism, such as the famous case of Joey, the mechanical boy. Or maybe his standards for "return to society" in an independent role are more lenient than those of others. Or it could be that the subtleties of his techniques have eluded other therapists struggling for success with these children.

In his book, unfortunately, we learn more of psychoanalytic inter-pretation than we do of his therapeutic technique. But at least he presents his ideas in a style less obscure than that of most psychoan-alytic writers, who appear to take exquisite pains in guarding the secrecy of their therapeutic insights. Consider, for example, the fol-lowing excerpt from a report of psychoanalytic treatment of a three-year-old girl diagnosed as psychotic:

> It is indeed striking how so many of the situations, in which we have reason to believe Alice was confronted with the potential shattering of her inner object world and with a concomitant depletion of the inner source of self, led directly to a primitivization of the thought process as exemplified by the shift from secondary process to primary process thought patterns, to an undermining of her reality sense and, very particularly, the sharp delineation of the primal modalities of inside and outside. The defensive and restitutive aspects of this inside-outside con-fusion, for example, are quite clear. When Alice was frantically look-ing around for something outside while, in fact, she was responding to the inner bowel urgency, the inside-outside confusion served to deny the imminence of the catastrophic loss of the stool object . . . . (167, p. 139)

Quite clear??

As Kanner (76) pointed out in his somewhat satirical article, "The Children Haven't Read Those Books," the hypotheses that Freud wise-ly presented in tentative, cautious fashion have been adopted as a "credo" by many of his disciples and accepted as "professed certainties and decreed verities." The use of psychoanalytic theory has obviated the need for careful diagnosis based on clinical observation of the child. Kanner referred to the famous child analyst, Melanie Klein, in illustrating his point:

> Melanie Klein, asserting not less than 9 times how "very clear" and "very obvious" it all was, could decide in an *unfinished* play analysis of 575 hours spread over 2½ years that 6-year-old Erna suffered from me-galomania, paranoia, pseudologia, severe depression, sadistic and can-nibalistic impulses, masochism, homosexual tendencies, and love

desires, and a desire to be seduced, all this held together by a "clearly" insatiable appetite for her father's penis and her mother's breasts. (p. 4)

Clancy's Treatment: Establishing a Bond

An earlier chapter noted that Bettelheim has a surprising theoretical ally in the ethologist Nikolaas Tinbergen (74), who agrees that autism is basically an emotional disorder and, as such, should be treated "at an emotional level." Tinbergen stresses the need for "therapies that aim at the reduction of anxiety and at a restarting of proper socialization" rather than therapies directed at "the teaching of specific skills," such as behavior modification, special education, and speech therapy. Bettelheim's approach represents, at least theoretically, the "treatment at an emotional level" advocated by Tinbergen but the methods developed by the Australian therapist Helen Clancy come closer to what Tinbergen is talking about.

Long before Tinbergen directed his attention toward autism, Helen Clancy (20) had begun to develop a method of treatment directed toward the establishment of proper socialization in the autistic child. Like Bettelheim, Clancy thinks that autism is an affective disorder, but there the similarity ends. Instead of using Freudian theory in her treatment of autism, Clancy draws heavily on the concepts and research findings of ethology, the study of animal behavior in its natural habitat. In order to better understand the rationale underlying her treatment, we should review some of these findings.

An earlier chapter referred to the ethologists' study of *critical periods* in the development of primary socialization in lower animals. The prototype for the critical period was demonstrated by Konrad Lorenz (168) in his fascinating studies of *imprinting* in birds. Lorenz used the term imprinting to denote the formation of a bond between the mother and the hatchling goose, duck, and other fowl. In his initial experiments, Lorenz showed that the gosling, shortly after hatching, follows the first moving object that comes into view and thereafter is attached to that particular object. Usually the first moving object in the gosling's natural environment is the mother goose; but when she is not there, the gosling "imprints" on another object if it happens to come along at the right time. This other object may be a wooden model of a goose drawn by a string or a tin can dangling from a conveyor belt or even Konrad Lorenz himself, flapping his arms, waddling, and honking like a mother goose. Such imprinting occurs within a critical period that does not go beyond three days after hatching; if the mother is absent during this period, the appropriate imprinting does not occur later, and the inappropriate imprinting is established permanently and ir-reversibly. So permanent is its effect that the gosling imprinted to a human being grows up to court humans as if trying to make them sexual partners.

Moving up the phylogenetic scale to higher mammals, we also find critical periods for primary socialization or bonding, although not so precisely manifested as in the imprinting of birds. Goats and sheep have served as good subjects for the study of the development of socialization because they, like humans, are truly social animals who develop strong attachments to one another and form societies. In fact, the adjective *gregarious*—which we apply to the most sociable humans and which represents the antithesis of the autistic child's behavior—is derived from the Latin phrase, "belonging to a herd or flock." In goats, the interaction involved in establishing a bond between the mother and newborn infant is quite intricate (169). The nanny begins licking the kid right after he is born, thereby waking him and causing him to stagger to his feet. There follows a reciprocal interaction be-tween the mother and kid that is highly ritualized. While licking the kid from nose to tail, the mother edges her body alongside his until his mouth almost reaches her nipple; before he can get the nipple in his mouth, though, she finishes licking his tail, turns around, and starts at his head again. This ritual continues for two hours or more until the mother finally remains still and permits the kid to nurse. Through this interaction a stable bond is formed between the nanny and the kid—a bond that serves as a foundation for the baby goat's later relationships with his mother and other goats.

If something goes wrong during this period of mother-infant in-teraction, however, the kid develops permanent problems in sociali-zation. Here is where the similarity to autism enters the picture. If the kid is separated from the nanny during the four hours or so fol-lowing birth and the ritual prevented, no bond between the two is formed. Or if the ritual is interrupted before it runs its course, the kid nurses and wanders away, his hunger satisfied. The next time he is hungry, though, he does not appear to recognize his own mother and randomly approaches other mother goats who butt him away. He is rebuffed even by his own mother, who does not appear to recognize him and refuses to let him nurse. The kid will starve to death unless human beings intervene and feed him; but even then, his abnormal development continues. If he stays with the flock, he shows various neurotic symptoms. If he is reared by humans, he remains alienated from goat society.

The ethologist J. P. Scott (170), who has studied critical periods for primary socialization in different mammals, has found that lambs who are separated from their mothers at birth and raised by humans also develop unusual social behavior, behavior that provides a striking parallel to that of autistic children. Rather than mingling with the herd, these sheep remain aloof and graze contentedly in solitary independence.

The research of ethologists such as Scott indicates, then, that there is a critical period in certain mammals during which a primary bond is formed between mother and infant. This bond, however, is not formed through a passive relationship between the two but rather through an active, give-and-take interaction. If the bond is not established during the critical period, permanent defects in socialization result. Although a critical period for primary socialization has not been clearly demonstrated in human development, Helen Clancy (20) thinks that some of the concepts derived from ethological research can be applied to autism and its treatment. She proposes that the basic problem in the autistic child is his failure to form a normal bond with his mother during infancy. Although Clancy proposes an organic predisposition toward autism, she thinks that the disorder can best be understood and treated as a developmental process that operates within the complex social system of the family. The relationship which is most critical in this process is the reciprocal interaction between the mother and infant, especially during the early feeding sessions. Since the autistic baby reportedly has problems in sucking, he may have more difficulty in responding positively to the mother during these sessions; he does not cuddle or experience the pleasant contact that serves as the foundation for the bond that develops readily in most infants. The feeding session is therefore an unpleasant experience for both the mother and the child. The mother senses the baby's lack of responsiveness and perhaps stiffens and alters her response to the child, thereby hindering further the development of the bond and reinforcing the autistic process. This process is reinforced more and more through other early interactions between the child and his mother and other family members. Clancy thinks, however, that the autistic process can be interrupted and a normal course of primary and secondary socialization can be established in the child. This is what her treatment is all about.

  While the focus of this chapter is on Clancy's treatment technique rather than any critique of her theory, it may be briefly interjected at this point that it is difficult to accept the idea that sucking problems play any critical role in the development of autism, especially when we look at other children with severe defects in sucking. About one child in 700, for example, is born with a cleft palate, a disorder that precludes normal sucking and creates formidable feeding difficulties. None of these children, however, has been reported to have autism.

  Clancy's mode of treatment contrasts markedly with that of Bettelheim. The therapist using Bettelheim's technique is passive and unobtrusive, allowing the child to express himself freely; the therapist using Clancy's technique is active and intrusive, directing and shaping the child's behavior with operant conditioning. Bettelheim's program excludes the mother from the treatment process; Clancy's program includes the mother as a vital participant.

  Clancy's treatment regimen is designed primarily for children no older than six. Its main objective is to establish affective bonds between the autistic child and members of his family, particularly the mother. Its secondary objective is to promote the learning of skills that facilitate socialization, such as language. The first step in forming a bond between the mother and child is the correction of the feeding problem. This problem, which is characterized in its earliest form by lazy sucking, may have hindered, as mentioned earlier, the formation of the attachment to the mother. In order to insure that the treatment program is rigorous and well-controlled, both mother and child are at first hospitalized, and the child is deprived of food so that food becomes a potent reward to him. At each successive meal the therapist offers the hungry child a new food, camouflaged by the preferred food. The food range of the child is thereby extended and, usually within one week, he begins to eat normally.

Under the guidance of the therapist, the mother then assumes the responsibility for feeding, and the feeding session becomes a playtime in which social reinforcement is paired with food. The session provides an opportunity for pleasant interaction between mother and child, an interaction that is well-planned and calculated to shape the social responsiveness of the child. The session includes such activities as water play, rough-and-tumble play, and bubble play. Exploiting the autistic child's attraction to round, shiny objects, the mother may blow bubbles to get the child's attention and engage him in play. At first the child, in typically autistic fashion, responds only to the bubbles rather than to his mother. Gradually, however, he discovers that he must meet certain demands in order to continue the play activity. He must, for example, show eye contact and make utterances if play is to be continued. Through this play interaction, the child becomes more and more receptive to physical contact, and the mother is encouraged to provide long periods of cuddling and physical comfort.

In order to facilitate the formation of attachment to the mother, the therapist may have to contrive situations in which the child is forced to respond negatively to strangers and seek emotional refuge in the mother. Clancy terms this the "wicked-witch, fairy godmother" approach. A normal infant develops a "stranger response" at about seven months of age; that is, he reacts to strangers with some anxiety and alarm. Some researchers think that the appearance of the stranger response signifies the completion of the primary socialization process between mother and child—the formation of the reciprocal bond between the two. Since no such bond has been formed between the autistic child and his mother, the child exhibits no stranger response under ordinary circumstances. The therapist, then, playing the role of the "wicked witch," frightens the child into retreating into his mother's protective arms. Through this technique, the child learns to view the mother as a positive figure, and the formation of an attachment to her is facilitated.

Through using these procedures, Clancy claimed that a therapist is "able to develop strong bonds between the mother and child in a period of about one month" (20, p. 239). These bonds are shown in a strong preference, previously absent, for the mother, the emergence of a "stranger response," a conspicuous change in the quality of emotions, and the spontaneous appearance of babbling in children who were previously silent. The child is expected to show some regression or "slippage" when he re-enters the normal family setting. The long-range goal of treatment, according to Clancy, is to develop bonds between the child and his whole family. In order to minimize regression in the child and promote affiliation with other members of the family, the program is intensively continued at home. The child also attends a daily program for autistic children after he is discharged from the hospital. In this program the staff ·and the mother continue the strengthening of affiliative responses in the child; the child also under-goes regular training in perceptual skills and speech.

In assessing the overall effectiveness of her program, Clancy reported that in all cases treated, the feeding aberrations have been eliminated and a normal diet established. Bonding has always been achieved between mother and child, with some satisfactory generalization to other family members. Language, according to Clancy, has been the area most resistant to treatment, with some children showing relatively rapid response to treatment and others showing little response.

While Clancy's approach shows promise, the final evaluation will come only with long-range follow-up studies of these children who have shown so far a favorable response to her program. For the ultimate test of any treatment is in terms of how well it helps the autistic child adjust to society and adapt to the real world as he grows older. Clancy admitted that the "greatest weakness in the overall approach is the relative lack of carry-over from the treatment situation to the family situation" (p. 241), and she reported that the positive carry-over to people outside the family is even less. This weakness, she stressed, can be overcome only through programs that "involve re-shaping of the total affiliative system within the family" (p. 241). How well this can be accomplished remains to be seen.

Breaking the Affective Barrier

Chapter 8 discussed the theory of autism developed by DesLauriers and Carlson in their book *Your Child is Asleep* (142). They have proposed that the autistic child suffers from an inborn imbalance in his arousal mechanism, which consists of two systems. System I, the reticular formation in the brain, serves to motivate or energize the normal person; System II, the limbic area of the brain, provides the substrate for feelings of pleasure, pain, and reward. These authors suggested that System II is generally too weak in the autistic child, creating a sensory and affective barrier that accounts for his cognitive and affective deficits. Their treatment, as the title of the book suggests, represents an attempt to awaken the autistic child through overcoming the affective barrier with intensive stimulation. They do not adhere to any one approach in their program but combine affection, control, tactile and kinesthetic stimulation, and behavioral techniques, which are discussed in the next chapter.

DesLauriers and Carlson stated that the barrier can be penetrated only if the autistic child is approached at a very basic level of sensory and affective stimulation. Since he tends to rely more heavily on the proximal senses in his learning, these senses should be exploited in the treatment. Further, two other conditions must be met in order for him to learn: (1) He must experience "excessive repetition" or "repeated encounters with the same stimulus situation" (p. 35). (2) He must experience the things to be learned within a strong affective or emotional context. In order for experiences to register with him, then, they must occur over and over with high emotional intensity.

Beyond these conditions, which are required for learning in all autistic children, these therapists specified different treatments for the "hyperactive" autistic child and the "hypoactive" one. The hyperactive or hypersensitive child should be given relatively mild stimulation through the proximal senses, which would include the senses of touch (tactile) and movement (proprioception and kinesthesis). The hypoactive and hyposensitive child, on the other hand, must be bombarded with stimuli through these same sensory channels—stimuli that are repetitious and have intense affective values.

DesLauriers and Carlson have reported improvements in most of the autistic children they have treated with such techniques. As with all other techniques, however, no cures were effected. Still their approach represents an admirable attempt to translate a comprehensive, well-formulated theory of autism into a sensitive, eclectic day-to-day program for the autistic child.

Although they think that the child has an underlying affective disorder, DesLauriers and Carlson, as well as Clancy, do not indict the parents or separate them from the child's treatment as Bettelheim does. Further, they use structured, direct techniques that Bettelheim believes limits the child's expression of self and ultimate freedom. Many of these techniques are based on learning principles and are variations of behavior modification, the controversial approach to treatment that is considered next.

11 Treatment at the Behavioral Level

The approaches that were considered in the last chapter all represent attempts to treat the autistic child through correcting a presumed affective disturbance or deficit. Bettelheim proposes that the autistic child has emotionally withdrawn from the rejecting world of his mother; in order to find himself, he must be treated in a totally acceptant environment. Clancy thinks that the autistic child has failed to form a primary bond with the mother; treatment, then, is directed at establishing a bond. DesLauriers and Carlson propose that the child has an innate affective barrier that must be overcome in treatment. Even though Clancy and DesLauriers and Carlson have incorporated behavioral techniques into their programs, they still think that the underlying defect in forming affective attachments must first be attacked before the child can show any significant or pervasive changes in behavior. Most behavior therapists disagree somewhat with them and even more with Bettelheim and the psychoanalysts.

As noted before, behavior therapists are more concerned with the present behavior of the autistic child and how it can be changed than with past history or presumed underlying causes and dynamics. In this respect, their philosophy of treatment represents the antithesis of traditional psychodynamic approaches, particularly psychoanalysis. The behaviorists differ from the psychoanalysts in other respects, too. Whereas the psychoanalysts are generally vague and well-insulated by cryptic language and theoretical circumlocutions, the behaviorists are precise and empirical, subject to a self-imposed scrutiny. In contrast to the method and theory of psychoanalysis, which is based on Sigmund Freud's clinical observations of a relatively small number of Viennese patients with Victorian sexual mores, the techniques of behavior therapy are founded most directly on the research in animal learning of the Russian physiologist Ivan Pavlov and the American psychologist B. F. Skinner.

Criticisms of Behavioral Techniques

From the time they started applying their techniques to human problems, the behavior therapists encountered resistance and criticism from professionals and the general public. Despite its success, behavior therapy is still under attack today. The psychodynamic therapists question the long-range effectiveness of behavior therapy on the grounds that it only temporarily eliminates symptoms which will reappear in other forms since the underlying problem is untreated; the behaviorists answer this criticism with empirical data that show that this "symptom substitution" does not occur. Some of the criticisms, however, cannot be answered with empirical data for they deal more with philosophical and ethical values.

One such criticism centers on the so-called dehumanizing effect of the conditioning techniques used in behavior therapy or behavior modification. We may conjure up with horror the infants of Aldous Huxley's *Brave New World* (171), who were conditioned to behave and think collectively like synchronized watches, or the assassin in Richard Condon's *Manchurian Candidate* (172), who was conditioned to kill like an automaton, or the young rapist in Anthony Burgess's *Clockwork Orange* (173), who was conditioned to recoil from the touch of a female. With these fictional victims of conditioning in mind, we may accuse the behavior therapists of exerting authoritarian control over the individual's behavior, thereby depriving him of his humanity and free will. We may say, as the critics have, that the human is being conditioned to respond in a mechanical, mindless manner like Pavlov's salivating dogs or Skinner's lever-pressing rats. While these criticisms raise valid questions about the limits to which conditioning techniques can ethically be taken, we should not throw out the baby with the bath water. Later in this chapter these ethical questions and how they relate to the use of behavior modification with autistic children are discussed more thoroughly. Before this, though, we need to have a clear understanding of what behavior modification is and how it has been applied to the problem of the autistic child.

Behavior Modification and the Autistic Child

The autistic child has been viewed as a special challenge by the behavior therapists. Here was a child who was largely unresponsive to traditional forms of psychotherapy and drug treatment, a child who presented behavior in the extremes, ranging from a very low frequency of social responses to a high frequency of maladaptive, stereotypic responses, a child who could not be maintained at home or school, a child who might bite a plug out of his arm or bash his head against a wall. Such a child would put behavior therapy to a severe test, and success with him would enhance broader acceptance of behavioral techniques as legitimate, useful therapeutic tools.

During the 1960s behavior treatment programs sprang up across the country and began to report promising results with autistic children. These programs used primarily the techniques of operant conditioning, to which the term "behavior modification" is applied most frequently. In Chapter 7 some of the basic principles and terms of operant learning were introduced in the discussion of Ferster's theory. The most fundamental principle is that the child's behavior is shaped by its positive or negative consequences. In behavior therapy using operant conditioning, you specify the behavior you want to change (the target behavior) and then systematically apply consequences when that behavior occurs in the child. If you want to accelerate the behavior or increase the frequency of its occurrence, you apply positive consequences, or rewards, in the form of primary or secondary reinforcers. If you want to decelerate or eliminate the behavior, you apply negative consequences either in the form of punishment or withdrawal of positive consequences (extinction). As you apply these consequences, you assess their effectiveness by measuring the behavioral change in the child.

This specification of "target behavior," systematic delivery of consequences, and measurement of behavior change distinguishes behavior modification from other forms of psychotherapy and allows for an objective, ongoing evaluation of the effectiveness of the treatment program. If certain reinforcers are found to be ineffective, then they can be abandoned and other reinforcers tried. With behavior modification, then, the program is constantly being assessed and adjusted according to the response of the child.

Behavior therapy with the autistic child has been directed primarily toward increasing his social responsiveness, teaching him useful skills, and decreasing maladaptive behavior, such as tantrums and self-abuse. One of the basic problems, however, is finding a positive reinforcer that works with him. Since such social rewards as smiles, praise, or pats-on-the-back have limited reinforcing value for the typical autistic child, the reinforcer at first is usually a primary one (119). Frequently, some form of food that can be doled out in small portions (such as pieces of candy or cereal or spoonfuls of ice cream) is used in the initial stages of treatment; these primary reinforcers then are repeatedly paired with social reinforcers in an attempt to build the strength of the latter.

An illustration of how this technique can be used to increase the frequency of a certain specified social behavior is the teaching of the response of eye contact—a response that occurs with very low frequency in the autistic child. In the first session, the therapist determines the "base rate" of eye contact in the child, that is, the number of times he looks directly at the therapist during a given period of time. During the early stages, the therapist may have to turn the child's face toward him or prompt him by saying, "Look at me, Johnny." Through the use of immediate candy reward—popped into the child's mouth right after he looks at the therapist—the frequency of eye contact is increased. At the same time the candy is given, the therapist may also smile and say, "Good, Johnny!" In this way, the smiles and praise assume meaning through their repeated associations with the primary reinforcement of candy and may later be used as social reinforcers by themselves.

The same techniques can be used to increase the frequency of other types of social behavior in the autistic child, such as responding appropriately to questions rather than echoing them. With complex patterns of behavior, such as speech, the therapist may have to use certain "shaping" and "chaining" procedures which involve breaking down the desired behavior pattern into component responses which are to be taught separately and then combined to form the pattern.

In shaping responses in the child, the therapist may have to use the technique of "successive approximations," selectively reinforcing those responses that approximate more and more closely the desired end result. For example, in teaching the autistic child to approach an adult, the therapist first reinforces the child for only turning toward her; once this response is established, the therapist withholds further reward until the child takes a step or two toward her, and so on.

In using operant conditioning with autistic children, it should be kept in mind that the reinforcer that works with one child may fail with another. Sometimes the therapist has to search around and experiment with a number of reinforcers before finding an effective one. In some cases, an activity that the child likes to engage in may be used as a reinforcer for a behavior that the therapist is trying to increase. The last chapter, for example, included a description of how Helen Clancy (20) uses bubble play as a reinforcer for eye contact and speech in some of the autistic children she treats.

First Operant Studies with Autistic Children

Until the 1960s the psychodynamic approach prevailed (and largely failed) in the treatment of autistic children. However, the appearance in 1961 of Ferster's behavioral analysis of autism served as a stimulus for research that tested the effectiveness of operant conditioning as a treatment technique with the autistic child. Ferster himself, along with Marian DeMyer (174), was the first to demonstrate that autistic children will perform certain simple tasks, such as pulling levers and solving matching problems, when reinforced. Although the performance of these tasks had little practical significance, these experiments showed that, if relevant reinforcers are used, the behavior of autistic children follows the principles of operant conditioning; that is, the behavior of these children can be shaped to some extent if certain consequences are programmed into their environment.

Other studies dealing with more practical problems followed. While most of these studies used only one subject, they were designed so that the effects of the treatment could be unequivocally interpreted. In one such study (175) operant conditioning was used to treat the everyday behavior problems presented by a three-and-one-half-year-old autistic boy; these problems included inappropriate eating habits, deficient social and verbal behavior, self-destructive behavior, and refusal to wear glasses which he needed in order to see. The boy showed striking initial improvement in these areas and continued to improve after discharge from the program to the extent of being able to participate in a public school program (176).

Since lack of meaningful speech is so typical of the autistic child and presents such a practical barrier to social interaction and adjustment, researchers were eager to see if operant conditioning could be used to build his communicative speech. Frank Hewett (177) was one of the first to develop a systematic procedure which used operant principles in teaching speech to an autistic child who was previously mute. Using shaping procedures, he first taught the child to attend to the therapist's modeling of speech elements; the child was then rewarded as he approximated and eventually matched the modeled speech. Through this procedure the child began to learn the rudiments of meaningful speech.

These early studies, while demonstrating that operant conditioning could be used to improve the behavior of autistic children, at the same time revealed some of the basic deficits present in these children. One such deficit that interferes greatly with the teaching of these children is their difficulty in learning by imitation or observation. In his highly influential research, Albert Bandura (178) has demonstrated that normal children learn a great deal of social behavior through observing and imitating the behavior of adults and peers. Such behavior is learned in the absence of any direct reward. Autistic children, for whatever reason, seem to learn very little in this manner. Special techniques had to be devised, then, to facilitate their imitative learning, and this is precisely what Metz (179) did. He showed how autistic children, who normally failed to imitate, could be taught to imitate nonverbal behavior by being reinforced for such imitation. Lovaas and his associates (180) then employed these operant learning principles to shape imitative verbal behavior in autistic children who were previously mute. This discussion now concentrates on the work of Lovaas, whose research and training programs have added immeasureably to our understanding of what can and cannot be accomplished through operant conditioning with the autistic child.

Lovaas's Behavior Modification Program

Ivar Lovaas of UCLA has done more than perhaps any other person in developing and testing operant conditioning programs for autistic children. He agrees with Ferster's notion that the autistic child has a deficit in ability to acquire social reinforcers. While the normal child acquires these reinforcers quite easily in most environments, the autistic child does not. This difficulty, Lovaas thinks, may be part of a broader deficit in learning to respond selectively to diverse environmental stimuli (181, 182). Lovaas's research has suggested that the autistic child has an "overselective" attention; that is, he responds rigidly to only one feature of a complex stimulus while ignoring other features. Lovaas (164) has argued that even though the autistic child may start life with this deficit, he should not be regarded as hopelessly beyond the reach of any therapeutic program. Like the blind child or deaf child, he needs to have a special learning environment arranged for him.

Lovaas claims no "cures" through the use of behavior therapy with autistic children. He does believe, however, that it has proven to be of more benefit than other approaches. In explaining the differential response to behavioral treatment shown by these children, Lovaas (183) invoked the image of a ladder with a hundred steps. One child may start at the fiftieth step and progress through treatment to the eightieth step. A child with a more severe impairment may start at the tenth step and progress to the thirtieth step. In both cases there is improvement, but there are differences in the starting point and the number of steps taken.

The ladder analogy applies even further to Lovaas's treatment program. The plan for each child is laid out in detailed step-by-step fashion; the therapy is, in Lovaas's words, "programmed learning in slow motion" which consists of systematic reward of appropriate behavior and immediate suppression of inappropriate behavior.

Development of Speech

One area that Lovaas and his associates have focused on is the development of meaningful speech in autistic children who were previously mute or whose speech was limited to echolalia. Lovaas (182) devoted an entire book to describing the careful procedures developed for building language skills in these children. He stated that when he started the program in 1964, he thought it best to ignore the theories linking the language impairment in autism to brain damage. "The prognoses one gathers from these arguments," he said, "are so pessimistic that one would be unlikely to start a language program if one attended to them" (p. 33). Instead, he assumed that the autistic child's deficient speech is due to a deficient motivational structure; the key, then, is to find the appropriate motivators, or reinforcers, that can be used to teach him meaningful speech.

In working with the mute autistic child, the first step involves training the child to imitate the speech of a model. Once the child can imitate, he becomes similar to speaking autistic children who use echolalia; he can parrot the speech of others without knowing the meaning. The next steps consist of imbuing speech with meaning through associating it with certain contexts or stimuli. In developing the expressive component, the child is reinforced for giving a verbal response to a nonverbal stimulus; he may, for example, be taught to label a food such as ice cream. In developing the receptive component (or comprehension), the child is taught to give a nonverbal response to a verbal stimulus, as in responding to the command, "Give me the book." Eventually, the expressive and receptive components are combined since most everyday situations involve both.

The program progresses from simple, concrete language to more abstract. It begins with teaching the child to label, the labeling being given some functional significance in the child's life. For example, when he appropriately uses the label "ice cream," he is reinforced with the ice cream. The child gradually moves on to learn pronouns, abstract time concepts, grammar, story telling, and conversational and spontaneous speech. Lovaas pointed out that these higher levels are only rarely achieved by autistic children who were initially mute; however, these levels are almost always reached by the children who started the program with echolalic speech.

Although the program concentrates on teaching the child language, it also stresses the shaping of his social and self-help skills. Lovaas and his co-workers (184) have described a procedure for building nonverbal imitation that is especially useful in the development of these skills. It includes techniques for instilling in the child those behaviors that make him more sociable and independent, such as greetings and displays of affection, feeding and dressing himself, brushing his teeth, and so on. The technique uses shaping methods that reward the child for making closer and closer approximations to the behavior modeled by the teacher. Through learning to discriminate the similarity between his behavior and that of the model, he in turn learns to imitate.

In evaluating his language program, Lovaas (182) reported that the child who starts out with some speech, even though it is echolalic, shows the most significant and durable improvement in language skills. In some cases, the gains can be quite dramatic. Linda, for example, entered the program at three years, four months of age with only echolalic speech; after twelve months of intensive treatment, her speech progressed to the point where she no longer needed the intensive program. Although she is still receiving therapy to help her converse more easily with her peers, Lovaas believes that "the differences between Linda and her peers are quite small" and that "a naive observer could not today single out Linda from among schoolmates as an exceptional child" (p. 230).

While children such as Linda generally show lasting benefits in language development from the program, the originally mute children do not fare as well. Lovaas stated that the primary weakness in the program is its failure to maintain a high rate of speech in these children. This failure, he proposed, may be related to the child's limited repertoire of social reinforcers and to his inability to control language, as the normal child presumably does, through intrinsic, self-stimulating reinforcers.

Elimination of Self-Abusive and Self-Stimulatory Behavior

Though Lovaas and his associates have helped autistic children make significant strides in language and other skills, perhaps the most successful, and controversial, feature of his program is the treatment of self-mutilation, which Lovaas regards as "one of the most bizarre and profoundly sick behaviors that one will ever encounter" (185, p. 296). This inexplicable behavior, characterized by fierce, relentless, repetitive attempts by the child to maim himself, may be carried to appalling and even life-threatening extremes. The child who once showed harmless head-banging in his crib may later beat his head over and over against a concrete wall so violently that he detaches his retina (185). One girl described by Lovaas (164) persisted in chewing her hands. She had bitten off the little finger of her left hand down to the second joint and had started on the little finger of the other hand. She also peeled off her fingernails with her teeth. One boy had chewed his right shoulder to where the bones could be seen. Other children have broken their noses with their knees.

Until recently the treatment for many of these self-mutilative children was to put them in full restraints—that is, bind them to a bed to protect them from themselves. Lovaas (164) reported that he had seen ten-year-old children who had been in such restraints for six or seven years. In exploring alternatives to this radical treatment, Lovaas and his associates discovered that this seemingly irrational behavior could be explained in terms of operant learning principles. If the self-destructive behavior is viewed as an expression of "a shattered, guilty, worthless self" and the child is accordingly given affection and sympathy when he commits it, then the behavior increases. On the other hand, if no such attention or reinforcement is given the child when he injures himself, then the behavior abates and over a period of time disappears. Lovaas (185) reported that when the children were put in a room and allowed to injure themselves without intervention from parents or nurses, the self-abusive behavior would gradually extinguish. Further, it was found that the child would not injure himself again in the particular room where extinction had occurred; but he would resume at a maximum level the self-mutilation in a situation only a few feet away if he had been given positive attention for such behavior there. In effect, the child had learned to discriminate the situation where he was reinforced for the behavior.

Lovaas pointed out, however, that this extinction procedure had severe limitations as a technique for eliminating self-abusive behavior, primarily because the child may injure himself severely in the slow process of reaching extinction. Then Lovaas happened on a more effective mode of treatment with a child whom he had come to regard more as his own child than as a patient:

> One day I was talking with her teacher and Beth began hitting her head against the edge of a steel cabinet. She would only hit steel cabinets and she would only hit them on the edge because, you see, she wanted to draw blood. Well, I think because I knew her so well, I just reacted automatically, the way I would have with one of my own children. I just reached over and cracked her right on the rear. She was a big, fat girl so I had an easy target. And I remember her reaction: "What the hell is going on? Is this a psychiatric clinic or isn't it?" (164, p. 79)

Lovaas admitted that while he felt "guilty" over hitting Beth, he also felt "great" because the self-destructive behavior had stopped for the moment. He knew then that Beth was capable of controlling it and that she would stop it when she knew that it would result in her being swatted.

> So I let her know there was no question in my mind that I was going to kill her if she hit herself once more, and that was pretty much it. She hit herself a few times after that, but we had the problem licked. One of the things that this taught me was that if you treat these kids like patients, you are finished. The best thing you can do is treat them like people. (164, p. 79)

Lovaas and his associates then began to develop techniques for the treatment of self-injurious children, using either spanking or non-harmful levels of electric shock as immediate punishment for such behavior (164, 185, 186). For milder forms of self-abuse, spanking has been successful. In more severe cases, shock has been used along with a strong reprimand: The therapist looks furious, shouts "No!" very loudly, and applies shock. Lovaas has found that with the application of shock, self-destructive behavior that has existed for years can be eliminated in a matter of minutes. He stressed, however, that the suppression of this behavior is specific to the situation in which the shock is applied; this means that the shock has to be applied in more than one environment. He reported, too, that he was both surprised and disappointed to find that the diminishment in self-destructive behavior is not accompanied by changes in large classes of other behaviors. "The children who stopped mutilating themselves," he stated, "did not simultaneously become normal" (185, p. 299).

The effective use of shock in eliminating self-abusive behavior in autistic children has been reported by a number of other researchers (e.g., 187, 188, 189). In a review of these studies, Lichstein and Schreibman (190) concluded that the positive side effects of the treatment greatly outweigh the negative ones. Nevertheless, this technique and other methods employing aversive contingencies continue to evoke heated debates among professionals and parents—debates that center on ethical issues that are considered shortly.

Recently other aversive measures have been used to control self-abusive behavior in autistic children. One such measure that may prove to be an effective alternative to shock is the forced inhalation of aromatic ammonia. Baumeister and Baumeister (191) reported that rapid, generalized, and durable suppression of self-injurious behavior was achieved in two children by administering ammonia fumes whenever the behavior occurred.

Evaluation of Behavior Modification Programs

In assessing those factors that contribute to the continued improvement of children who have been in their programs, Lovaas and his associates (183) reported that those children whose parents are trained and willing to conduct such treatment at home continue to show progress, whereas children who are put in institutions regress. One of the critical features of more successful parents is a willingness to apply strong, tangible consequences, such as food and spankings, to the child's behavior. Another characteristic is their rejection of the notion that their child is "ill;" instead of treating him as a sick person, they place some demands on him. They are also willing to commit a major part of their lives to their child and the daily management of behavior contingencies for him.

Although behavior therapy has been hailed by some as the panacea for autism, most persons using behavior modification with these children are acutely aware of its limitations. In reviewing the shortcomings of his program, Lovaas wrote:

> The most significant disappointment was the failure to isolate a "pivotal response," or, as some might describe it, the failure to effect changes in certain key intervening variables. This means that in the beginning, we searched for one behavior which, when altered, would produce a profound "personality change." We could not find it. We had hoped, for example, that when a child was taught his name ("My name is Ricky") that his awareness of himself (or some such thing) would emerge. It did not. Similarly, the child who learned to fixate visually on his therapist's face did not suddenly discover people. Our treatment was not a cure for autism. But we had to start somewhere. At least the child who learned his name was then in a position to learn someone else's name. When he learned to fixate visually on his therapist's face, he could pay more attention to teaching cues. (183, pp. 160-161)

The results of studies done by Lovaas and others indicate that behavior modification, although certainly not a cure for autism, does serve as the most effective means available for improving the behavior of autistic children. Self-injurious behavior can usually be eliminated or at least significantly reduced by extinction procedures (that is, by withholding attention) or by punishment. Social and self-help skills can be developed with behavior modification in nearly all autistic children, and language and academic skills improved in many. The progress of any child depends, of course, on the particular pattern of abilities and disabilities that he starts with.

Remembering the evidence reviewed in an earlier chapter on possible causes of autism, we may at this point ask the question: If autism appears to have an organic basis, then why bother with behavior modification when it does nothing about the cause? The answer is that such programs are not presumed to be cures for autism. But at least they do produce some positive change in the child, making him more manageable and more responsive to social and educational stimuli. As Rimland (125) has stated, operant conditioning can be effectively used to teach a child with Down's Syndrome to read, although it is certainly no cure for the condition.

Ethical Issues Concerning Behavior Modification

After this look at the techniques of behavior modification and their application to autistic children, we may return to the ethical questions referred to earlier in this chapter. The frequent criticism that autistic children are being relentlessly conditioned to respond like rats in a Skinner box and deprived of their humanity is not justified in most cases. Behavior modification, like any other treatment, can be abused and taken to unethical extremes in the hands of the wrong person. The techniques, as B. F. Skinner stated in his book *Beyond Freedom and Dignity* (192), are "ethically neutral" and "can be used by villain or saint." For this reason, behavior modification should be used with appropriate safeguards by well-trained, responsible professionals who have the child's total welfare in mind, and it should be used only with the consent and participation of the parents.

It is ironic that many of the parents and professionals creating the brouhaha over behavior modification condone much more readily other techniques that may be misleading, ineffective, or even harmful.

The methods of behavior modification are probably more humane than trying to subdue the child's behavior with excessive drug therapy or wasting the parents' money and time in lengthy psychodynamic treatment programs based on unfounded assumptions about the cause of autism. Whether explicitly stated or not, the long-range goal of any treatment program with autistic children is to beneficially influence the behavior of the child. The basic question, then, is which techniques are most effective in doing this.

In using conditioning in behavior modification, nothing new or mysterious is being done to deprive the individual of his humanity. Every human being is subjected to a variety of conditioning forces throughout his lifetime, forces that are usually beyond his control and often operating in disorganized, uncontrolled fashion. Some forces, however, may be well-planned by other people and designed to influence his behavior for their profit. Most parents rarely object to the barrage of TV commercials intermingled with the cartoons every Saturday morning, commercials carefully contrived to motivate the child to buy (or persuade his parents to buy) a certain cereal, a certain candy, a certain drink.

All of us experience conditioning, too, in our everyday interactions with other people. This conditioning is a natural inevitable part of life. For centuries, effective parents and teachers have used it to motivate children and promote learning. But it was only recently that the methods were studied scientifically and used formally in teaching and treatment programs. With behavior modification, the conditioning is done in systematic fashion with explicitly stated goals. Such conditioning, rather than being done in any underhanded way, should be above-board, with the parents actively contributing to the planning and conducting of the program. In using behavior modification with the autistic child, then, the parents and professionals show concern enough and take time enough to study carefully the child's behavioral problems and deficits so that they can plan a consistent, individualized program—a program designed to help the child to do more for himself and adjust better to society. Instead of turning the child into a trained animal or robot, the program strives to reduce his maladaptive behaviors and teach him new behaviors that will allow him to move more freely in the world.

Another criticism focuses on the use of punishment, such as spanking or electric shock, to eliminate undesirable behavior in the child. Such punishment, the critics say, is especially inhumane because the autistic child does not comprehend what he is being punished for. If aversive measures or punishment are used extensively and indiscriminately with autistic children, then the critics may have a stronger argument. Usually punishment is employed as a last resort to reduce behavior that is interfering markedly with his adjustment or endangering his physical health. It usually is applied when all other methods have failed, and milder forms of punishment such as reprimands or spankings are tried before shock is used. Whether to use shock, then, becomes a matter of weighing the risks against the benefits. Most of the studies, as noted earlier, strongly support the conclusion that the positive side effects outweigh the negative (190). When a child is persistently bashing his head against a wall at the risk of cracking his skull and damaging his brain, the application of shock to eliminate this behavior appears to be the lesser of two evils. It may appear to be a drastic measure, but when we consider the more drastic consequences of self-destructive behavior, we must concede that shock is the more humane alternative. It appears to be a more humane alternative, too, than keeping a child tied in bed for years in order to protect him from himself.

Many people erroneously associate the use of shock for self-destructive behavior in autistic children with the electroshock therapy employed in the treatment of psychiatric patients. Aside from using electricity, the two techniques bear no resemblance. The shock in the former case is not applied to the brain and does not induce convulsions; it is localized and harmless, although unpleasant to the child. A safeguard used in some treatment facilities requires that the person administering the shock must first experience the shock himself and allow the parents to also feel the level of shock. It is strange that many of the same parents who object strenuously to the use of harmless shock with their child blithely permit drug therapy with its possible harmful side effects.

Rimland (193) related that when he speaks to groups of parents about operant conditioning, someone invariably raises a question about the brutality involved in certain aversive methods, such as those used by Lovaas and his associates at UCLA and described in an article in *Life* magazine. He told how he handles this question:

"If you think that the children in the *Life* article were mistreated, you should see what they do to the kids at UCLA only two floors away in that very same building!" (Pause for effect.) "They don't just yell at the kids or slap them once in a great while. In that same building there are people who actually gas children and cut them with sharp knives." The audience would gasp and stare at me with disbelief.

"Well," I would say after a suitable pause, "How else are you going to do an appendectomy or a tonsillectomy?" (p. 101)

The critics of behavior modification tend to stress its use of negative consequences such as punishment and overlook its emphasis on positive motivation. Punishment and other aversive measures are probably used less in behavior modification than they are in society at large. Most parents spank their children, at one time or another, or reprimand them or deprive them of privileges in trying to influence their behavior. While these techniques may be used in behavior modification, they are used sparingly and with much less frequency than positive reinforcers in most programs.

Behavior modification has survived the criticism and is now an accepted part of most treatment and educational programs for autistic children and their parents. As the discussion now turns to some of these new programs, it should be noted that one of the most thoughtful defenses of behavior modification is provided in a "white paper" prepared in 1975 by the National Society for Autistic Children, an organization composed mainly of parents who themselves have participated in various types of treatment programs. The gist of this paper is that behavior modification, despite its limitations and possible abuses, is an extremely effective means of helping the autistic child and his family (194).

12 New Directions in Treatment

Regardless of the amount of specialized attention given the autistic child by professionals, any treatment or educational program is futile without the cooperation and involvement of the parents. As noted in the last chapter, those autistic children who show the most durable and generalized benefit from behavior modification are those whose parents are willing to implement treatment programs at home. Further, such home treatment appears to be much more effective in improving the behavior of the child if it is started when the child is quite young. Rather than being excluded from the treatment program, then, parents are becoming more and more the primary therapists for their child.

In order to enlist vital aid of the parents in the treatment of the autistic child, professionals must first offer to them help and understanding. Rather than implicating the parents, intensifying their guilt, and recommending therapy for their presumed personality problems, the professional should provide realistic information, practical guidance, and supportive counseling to help the parents in rearing their autistic child.

General Counseling of Parents

Eric Schopler (195), who has had considerable experience in working with parents in his program for autistic children at the University of North Carolina, has called attention to three problems that the professional should consider when counseling parents about autism. First, the professional should try to dispel the confusion that parents experience when confronted with the diagnosis of autism. Much of this confusion derives from "myth beliefs" about child rearing, beliefs perpetuated in society by professionals whose conclusions are based more on theory than empirical evidence. One such myth is the psychoanalytically based notion that autism is the result of an "unfavorable emotional climate in the family." Since many diagnostic evaluations are couched in psychoanalytic explanations of how family dynamics have produced the autistic child, the diagnostic records are vigilantly kept from the parents' eyes. Professionals have also refrained from showing the parents records because they contain information that might be unsettling to the parents, such as reports of brain damage. IQ scores, rather than being explained to the parents, are guarded as "top secret" and sacrosanct. Schopler suggested that the parents' confusion about autism can be reduced if the professional frankly discloses and interprets diagnostic information, including unpleasant elements, and admits the lack of clear knowledge regarding many aspects of autism.

A second problem that should be dealt with in counseling, according to Schopler, is the set of erroneous expectations that parents usually show in planning the future of their autistic child. Although parents often can estimate accurately their child's level of functioning in social, cognitive, motor, and self-help areas, they frequently fail to realize the long-range implications of their child's impairment in these areas. Because they may have been told that the autism in their child, and the resulting retardation in his intellectual functioning, is the result of social withdrawal, they may expect that the autism can be reversed through vaguely defined emotional experiences. The chances of this happening are quite small. The parents' hopes also may be elevated unrealistically by the array of treatment options now available, some highly touted by zealous proponents. The professional should avoid making exaggerated claims about any treatment or promises about cures that are unlikely to come. Instead, he should give the parents realistic long-range expectations based on the available information on the individual child, such as IQ scores and other data that yield valid predictions. The next chapter considers some of these early signs that are related to later adjustment in autistic individuals.

A third problem in parental counseling is the traditional conflict in roles between professionals and parents—a conflict that interferes with the effective treatment of the autistic child. The professional has traditionally assumed the role of the "authority," providing the "expert" knowledge but having no responsibility for the day-to-day problems posed by the child. The parents, on the other hand, traditionally have had the responsibility for rearing the child and meeting his everyday needs. Schopler advocates a merger of the two roles. The parents are usually experts about their own child and can provide useful and valid information to the professional. They can also participate actively in the treatment and education of the child, rather than leaving such functions completely in the hands of the professional. The professional, in turn, should share some of the responsibility and "accountability" for the child's overall welfare and should work to assure that appropriate treatment and special educational programs are available in the community.

The TEACCH Program

More and more it is evident that the most effective treatment programs for autistic children are those that are not bound by any one theoretical orientation or traditional approach. The most productive programs are those that flexibly incorporate recent research findings and proven techniques into a comprehensive whole—a whole that includes tested principles of behavior modification and special education, parental counseling and participation, useful diagnostic methods, and treatment that pervades the child's total life. One program that serves as an exemplary and innovative model for the development of comprehensive, community-based services to autistic children and their parents is the TEACCH program (Treatment and Education of Autistic and related Communications handicapped CHildren) in North Carolina. As noted in the last chapter, those autistic children who stay with involved parents fare much better than those who are sent to institutions. The TEACCH program provides an alternative to the traditional placement of autistic individuals in large state institutions by striving to keep the child with his parents and, as he grows older, within the community.

Eric Schopler and Robert Reichler of the University of North Carolina, who have been responsible for the development of the

TEACCH program, have reviewed the principles and philosophy underlying the program in various writings (e.g., 195, 196). First and foremost is the assumption, based on current research, that autism is a biogenic disorder and that the parents of autistic children have essentially normal personalities and do not provide pathogenic home environments. The problems that the parents do show in child-rearing are generally the result of the inevitable frustrations and difficulties in coping every day with an autistic child. Further, it has been found that the parents usually have a good grasp of the nature and extent of the child's handicap without, however, fully comprehending the long-range implications. The program is based on the principle, then, that treatment is enhanced when all that is known about the child and autism is completely and candidly shared with the parents. The parents, rather than being viewed as causal agent and therefore separated from the child's treatment, work hand-in-hand with the professionals toward the common goal of helping the child. The program also assumes that treatment of the autistic child is done most productively in a setting that is well-structured and educationally oriented—a setting that devises an individualized program aimed at helping the child and his family live together more effectively. Finally, instead of viewing the child as educationally hopeless and outside the purview of public education, the program assumes that the autistic child can be educated most effectively in special classes in public school in his community.

The child referred to the TEACCH program is first evaluated at one of three diagnostic and treatment centers, which are located in the three major population regions of North Carolina. During the first diagnostic visit, which usually lasts about four hours, the child is seen for a psycho-educational evaluation while both of his parents are interviewed by a staff member. The parents are also requested to bring toys and other play material from home that the child is familiar with. They then are observed in interacting with the child in a play situation using these materials. Such observation aids the staff in understanding the child's relationship with persons who are most familiar to him. When the initial evaluation is completed, the staff shares with the parents all diagnostic impressions and findings, answers questions, and makes recommendations.

When the initial study shows that the child may benefit from participation in the program, the family is given appointments during a trial period lasting six or eight weeks. This trial period offers parents the opportunity to learn what the program expects of them and what they, in turn, can expect from the program so that a realistic commitment can be made. At the end of this period, the findings and recommendations are discussed again with the parents. If it is agreed that the child and parents should continue in the program, a contract is made which specifies the working relationship between the parents and staff; this contract is reviewed at regular intervals for possible renewal. Reichler and Schopler (196) believe that even if the parents discontinue participation after the trial period, they usually depart with a better understanding of their child and how to manage him.

Depending upon the individual needs of the child and his family, the child's program may consist of treatment through the regional clinical center, placement in one of the TEACCH special education classes in his community, or a combination of both.

Diagnostic and Treatment Program

The TEACCH diagnostic procedures are highly pragmatic and unrelated to any particular theory. They are designed to yield information that can be readily translated into an individualized treatment and educational program for each child.

Each child is evaluated at the clinical center with the Psychosis Rating Scale (197) to estimate the degree of psychosis. Then he is assessed with the Psycho-educational Profile (PEP), an evaluation instrument developed from task items that have proven to be useful in teaching autistic children in the TEACCH program (196). The PEP is composed of five major scales that measure imitation (vocal and motor), sensory modalities (vision and hearing), motor development (fine, gross, and visual-motor integration), cognitive functions (auditory, vocal, and advanced), and language (imitation, vocabulary, verbal comprehension, reading, and visual comprehension). The PEP has an additional "Pathology Scale" which assesses unusual patterns of development in emotional, social, and behavioral areas including affect, relating, cooperation, human interest, play, and pathological sensory modes. The PEP yields a profile that depicts each child's particular strengths and weaknesses and allows for development of a treatment program that focuses on his individual needs independent of any professional and theoretical issues.

The TEACCH program departs from tradition in several aspects of its treatment program. First, the therapists who work with the children and their parents are not highly trained and specialized professionals but instead come from diverse educational backgrounds ranging from linguistics to Chinese art. They are hired as therapists not on the basis of their educational background or professional identity but for their interest and sensitivity in helping autistic children and their parents. As Reichler and Schopler (196) put it, "occupational investments, identity, and training often create biases and limitations that make the specialist respond in terms more of his specialized knowledge than of the needs of an individual child and his family" (p. 360).

Each staff member functions in the dual role of providing therapy to children and consultation to parents, though typically not with the same family. This gives the staff member a more balanced perspective on parent-child interactions and moderates any biases toward either parents or children. He or she tends to accept the parents as reasonable people who are genuinely trying to cope with an extremely difficult problem; the parents, in turn, accept the therapist and the program with fewer defenses and a stronger commitment toward implementing the therapist's suggestions, which may sometimes be demanding and difficult. "The overall effect" according to Reichler and Schopler (196), "is one of mutual acceptance and identification between parent and therapist as people with a shared experience and some knowledge of what it is like to be in the other's position" (p. 360).

Another departure from tradition in the TEACCH program is the enlistment of the parents as co-therapists. Rather than being isolated from the child's therapy, as they are in most traditional programs, the parents assume responsibility for much of the treatment. When the child is accepted into the program, the parents agree to collaborate in treatment for a definite period of time. This collaboration requires that they regularly attend sessions in which they observe the therapist's demonstration, discuss problems with their parent consultant, or demonstrate the home program for their child.

The parents' participation as co-therapists involves both observation of therapy demonstrations and implementation of a home treatment plan. The therapy demonstrations are arranged so that the parents and their parent consultant observe through a one-way screen the actual treatment session with their child, with the consultant directing their attention toward relevant features of the demonstration and answering their questions. The focus of the session is agreed upon in advance by the therapist and the parent consultant who has, in turn, conferred with the parents on particular problems they may need help with. The parents may report, for example, difficulty in controlling the child's behavior; the therapist, then, may demonstrate methods for maintaining better control.

Along with the observation sessions, parents are given home programs individually designed for their child. These programs, which are revised at regular intervals, outline objectives, methods, and materials for working with the child in daily sessions. The specific content of the child's program is determined jointly by the therapist and parents. Once the program is underway, the parents are required, at regular intervals, to demonstrate it with their child while the consultant and therapist observe. As the parents gain experience, they become more and more resourceful and independent in maintaining and revising the home program. Reichler and Schopler (196) reported that many parents, particularly mothers, have developed into highly effective and innovative teachers.

Special Education Program of TEACCH

In addition to the treatment offered through the clinical centers, the TEACCH program provides special educational services to the autistic child. Special education classrooms are distributed strategically throughout the state within community public schools. Each of the self-contained classrooms is designed to provide an individualized developmental program for five to eight children. If the child is capable, he is allowed to participate in certain activities in the regular classroom. Since the special education class also serves as a resource room for other children in the regular school program, the autistic child is exposed each day to the behavior of his normal peers.

Although the child in the special class may continue to receive treatment at the clinical center, he also gets a great deal of therapy along with his education within the context of the classroom program. The staff of each classroom, a teacher and assistant teacher, are especially trained by TEACCH to deal with the problems presented by the autistic child. Teachers, parents, and the center staff all contribute to such decisions as when the child will be enrolled and how long he will stay each day in the program. While most children attend for a full school day, some children require adjustments according to their developmental level. Parents maintain involvement through direct participation in the classroom and implementation of home programs. Parents can also attend regular meetings at each clinical center to meet each other, discuss common problems and experiences, and broaden their knowledge of autism through educational programs including films and speakers.

One concern that the TEACCH program has addressed recently is that of the need to provide services to the growing population of autistic adolescents (198). As the next chapter notes, the basic handicaps associated with autism persist in adolescence and adulthood. Instead of relegating autistic persons to large state institutions, as has been frequently done in the past, communities need to develop appropriate vocational training programs and employment opportunities for these individuals. Alternatives to institutional placement should be explored, such as the community group homes for adolescents developed through the TEACCH program. As Sloan and Schopler (198) pointed out, the basic goals for autistic adolescents should be the same as those for nonhandicapped persons of this age: "They must learn to get along with others; they must seek an occupation; they must take up a residence of their own and be responsible for their personal concerns such as health and sexuality" (p. 189).

Other Forms of Treatment

All of the treatment methods considered thus far have primarily been psychological, behavioral, or educational. To complete this discussion of interventions, some mention should be made of drug treatment and other forms of biochemical therapy used with autistic children.

Although a number of different drugs have been tried, none has eliminated the basic symptoms of autism. Some, however, have been successfully used in partially controlling some of the other problems frequently found in autistic children, such as hyperactivity, distractibility, stereotypic behavior, and sleep disturbances (3, 199). These drugs generally are employed when behavioral treatment has proven to be ineffective by itself; in all cases, however, drug therapy should be used only as an adjunct to other treatment programs. As Campbell, Geller, and Cohen (199) concluded in their critical review of drug research and treatment with autistic children, the paucity of well-controlled studies precludes any clear statements regarding how much drugs help autistic children.

A recent development in biochemical treatment that has engendered some controversy is the so-called megavitamin therapy. Some researchers (e.g., 200) have reported that some autistic children, particularly the classically autistic ones, show improvement in behavior with high doses of single or multiple vitamins. While this approach shows promise, the results are still inconclusive and further research is needed.

In closing this discussion of treatment methods, it should be stressed that the coverage of the different approaches and programs devised for autistic children has been necessarily selective. An entire book of considerable size could be devoted to the topic and still not exhaust it. At this stage, it looks as if the most effective treatment is that which incorporates highly structured behavioral and educational programs into all aspects of the child's life; even then, however, no cure is effected.

Lest the next chapter create pessimism about the outcome of autism in adolescence and adulthood, we must keep in mind that most of the treatment programs, such as TEACCH, have been developed only in recent years, and their long-range effectiveness has not been fully tested. This is especially true of the therapeutic and educational programs that intervene very early in the lives of young autistic children. We should remember, too, that a number of research projects, ranging from behavioral to biochemical, are currently being conducted. Perhaps this research will yield answers that will aid us in developing more effective preventive and treatment programs—programs that will cast a more optimistic light on the prospects of the autistic child.

13 Adolescence and Adulthood

The question that eventually enters the minds of most people interested in autistic children is: What happens to them as they grow up? This question may be prompted in some by natural curiosity about what happens to these strange and appealing children when they leave childhood; in others, the question may be stimulated by scientific interest or professional concern. To parents of an autistic child, however, this question becomes an intensely personal one because they, like most parents, entertain special hopes for his future. These hopes are often fired by the flickers of intelligence they see, or by claims for cures by zealous or exploitative practitioners, or by reassurances from friends, relatives, and even professionals that he will "outgrow the problem." Unfortunately, many parents painfully see their hopes dampened as the child grows older. The flickers of intelligence fail to coalesce into any sustained glow, the claims for cures take on a phony ring, and the reassurances that he will outgrow the problem diminish in frequency and conviction with each birthday. The question, then, of what the child will be like as an adult begins to loom even larger in the parents' minds. Sooner or later they begin to abandon many of their false hopes and start to search for straight answers.

Straight answers to these questions about long-range expectations, however, are extremely difficult to provide. The only basis for answers is the available data we have on autistic individuals who have already reached adolescence and adulthood. From such data we try to ferret out those characteristics that appear to be associated with long-term improvement and adjustment. The answers based on such data, though, must be viewed as tentative and should not be applied unequivocally to today's autistic child since many of the individuals studied, especially those who are now adults, did not have the benefit of the intensive early treatment and educational programs now available in some communities. Nevertheless, these are the only answers available at the moment.

Kanner's Follow-Up Studies

The first information on long-range prognosis appeared in 1971 when Kanner published his long-awaited study of the adult status of the original eleven autistic children seen in his Johns Hopkins Clinic (201). Twenty-eight years had passed since the children had first been described by Kanner in his classic paper on autism, and many people were eager to learn how they were faring as adults. Kanner's report, however, was not at all encouraging.

Out of the eleven, who were in their thirties at the time of the study, only two were able to function gainfully in society. One of these happened to be Donald, who, as noted in the introduction to Part I, was seen as a five-year-old by Kanner in 1938, representing the first "official" case of infantile autism. At the time of the follow-up study, Donald was thirty-six years of age and living as a bachelor with his parents in his hometown. He earned a college degree in French at twenty-four years of age and since then has worked as a teller in the local bank with no desire for promotion. He is somewhat active in civic and church affairs, having served, for example, as president of the Kiwanis Club. He is an avid golfer, playing four or five times a week and winning six trophies in local competition; he also is described as a fair bridge player, although he never initiates a game. His lack of social initiative, according to his mother, appears to be his most significant problem. He engages very little in social conversation and has demonstrated no interest in the opposite sex. In a report to Kanner, his mother stated that although Donald is "not completely normal," he has participated in society much better than his parents had ever hoped he would.

Frederick, the other member of the group who has maintained

gainful employment, was thirty-four years old at the time of follow-up; he was single and living at home with his parents. He has been employed full-time as a duplicating machine operator in a government office; he is viewed by his supervisor as very dependable and thorough in his work and considerate toward his fellow workers. According to his parents, when the family moved to a new home, he became acquainted with the neighbors and paid visits to them. One of his chief interests has always been music, and recently he has taken up bowling.

Although Donald and Frederick may not have achieved complete normality, especially in intimate social relations, they certainly have fared better as adults than the other nine members of the original group, all of whom at the time of follow-up were either in institutions or in highly sheltered settings. Kanner noted that there was nothing in the family backgrounds, parental personalities, developmental histories, or physical and psychological findings of these individuals that would have served to predict this outcome.

One year later Kanner and his associates (202) reported the results of a much more extensive follow-up study of the ninety-six children, now in their twenties and thirties, who were diagnosed as autistic at the Johns Hopkins Clinic before 1953. The results were equally disheartening. Out of the ninety-six (which included the original eleven reported on above), only eleven were capable of functioning productively in society as adults, and the rest were in sheltered or institutional settings.

The educational accomplishments of the eleven (ten males, one female) who had "emerged" to achieve adjustment were varied: three had college degrees; three had completed junior college; one was doing well in college; one had finished high school and another the eleventh grade; one had attended a private boarding school for exceptional children; and one had received vocational training in a sheltered workshop. Their current occupations were also diversified. As mentioned above, Donald was a bank teller and Frederick a duplicating machine operator. The occupations of the other nine were that of lab technician, accountant, "blue-collar" worker at an agricultural research station, general office worker, page in the foreign language section of a library, bus boy in a restaurant, truck loading supervisor, helper in a drug store, and college student. Two had previously joined the armed services but were honorably discharged within a year. In the area of social adjustment and independence, eight of the eleven were living by themselves, and the other three with their families. All had been relatively unsuccessful in trying to form personal friendships, and none had married or even seriously considered it.

In looking at the backgrounds of the eleven "successful" autistic adults, Kanner found that they had three things in common. First, all of them had used some speech before the age of five. Since some of the "unsuccessful" adults had also used speech before this age, this could not be regarded as an infallible prognostic sign. This early use of language could nevertheless be viewed as necessary, if not sufficient, for later adjustment.

The second common finding in these eleven "successful" adults was that none had spent any time in a state hospital or residential facility for the retarded. All had spent at least their preschool years at home and some a number of years longer. Three were still living with their families and the others saw their relatives regularly. As with the early language, staying out of an institution appeared to be necessary but not sufficient for adjustment, since many of the other autistic children had also stayed at home but had not achieved adjustment. Before indicting separation from parents and placement in an institution as negative influences, we should consider another point: It is likely that those cases who were referred to institutions were the most severely impaired in the first place. Their lack of later adjustment, then, may have been related more to the severity of their preinstitutional impairment than to the effects of being in an institution.

The third factor related to "success" was found only in the eleven who had "emerged." It had to do with the gradual change in "self-concept"—or the child's awareness of himself and his differences from others—as he grew older. During the years of early and middle childhood, there appeared to be little differences in the self-concept of the child who would later emerge and the one who would not. In this stage the child showed no awareness of being different and was content to "do his own thing" without relating to people. He reacted intolerantly to any interference with his self-contained existence. As he grew older, he began to tolerate more of these intrusions and began to emerge mechanically in some social rituals.

As the children entered their teens, however, Kanner reported that a "remarkable change" occurred in the eleven—a change that failed to occur in the others. They began to painfully sense their inherent difficulties in relating to people and made a deliberate, conscious attempt to compensate for these difficulties. They intensified their efforts as they grew older. Although they had difficulty with the "emotional" components of social interaction, they appeared to know "intellectually" what certain social expectations were. They therefore learned to go through the appropriate motions to establish contact with people and conform to these expectations. These contacts, however, did not develop into close friendships or intimate relationships. Through their painful awareness, though, they did compensate enough to make an adjustment to society.

Rutter's Follow-Up Studies

Several other comprehensive studies have been done on later adjustment of autistic children and the early factors that seem to relate to it. In 1967 the English psychiatrist Michael Rutter (203) reported such a study on sixty-three children who had been followed at Maudsley Hospital. These children were initially seen before puberty and were five to fifteen years older at the time of the follow-up report. Rutter found that the original IQ scores of these children served as significant indicators of later success. For those children who were untestable or had IQ scores below fifty, the prospect was rather dismal. Almost none acquired speech or received any schooling. Further, at the time of follow-up, three-fourths were in long-term hospitals.

Like Kanner, Rutter also found early speech to be a significant predictor for later adjustment. If the child failed to show useful speech by age five, the chances of recovery were very small. The amount of schooling that the child had received also seemed to be positively related to adjustment in adolescence. Both of these factors, of course, are related to the IQ of the child.

Out of the sixty-three children, only one was considered "normal" at adolescence, while eight had achieved a "good" adjustment and sixteen a "fair" adjustment. Most of the rest were incapable of any kind of independent existence and were in institutions. When marked improvement took place, it usually started before the age of six or seven years. From middle childhood on, the course was fairly consistent, either in the direction of improvement or deterioration. As in Kanner's group, improvement did not appear to be associated with traditional psychotherapy or prescribed professional treatment.

In subsequent follow-up studies Rutter (73) has found that twenty-eight percent of autistic individuals who revealed no clinical evidence of neurological disorder in early childhood have developed epileptic seizures by eighteen years of age. His studies also indicated that about seventy-five percent of all autistic individuals continue to function within the retarded range on intelligence tests throughout their lives. Further, those who show seizures or other signs of specific brain dysfunction tend to eventually function at the most impaired level.

DeMyer's Follow-Up Studies

In a follow-up study published in 1973, Marian DeMyer and her associates (204) at the Indiana University Medical Center examined the progress of a hundred and twenty autistic children whose average age was five-and-a-half years at the original evaluation and twelve years at the time of follow-up assessment. Most of the children remained educationally retarded and, as in Rutter's group, almost half, forty-two percent, had been placed in institutions. Out of the hundred and twenty, only two were viewed as functioning normally. Up to about twenty-five percent had achieved adjustment that was described as "fair" to "border-line" whereas about seventy-five percent had adjustment ratings of "poor."

DeMyer then looked at the "top twenty" children—those children who had achieved the highest adjustment ratings—to see what early factors distinguished them from the others. The two who had "recovered" did not differ significantly on the initial measures from the other eighteen in the "successful" group. However, the "top twenty" differed from the other one hundred children on these early measures. The most reliable early predictor was the child's rating on samples of work-school tasks. This finding is not surprising since the child was being rated on tasks representative of the work that he would later be required to do. The second best predictor was the Performance IQ of the child, that is, an IQ based on the child's ability to perform standardized tasks requiring perceptual and motor skills and nonverbal reasoning. The third best predictor was the severity of the disorder at the time of initial diagnosis.

DeMyer also found, as Rutter had, that very few of the autistic children showed an increase in IQ as they grew older. Pursuing this notion further in another study, she and her associates (205) investigated the stability of IQs in autistic children and the relationship the IQ had to the outcome of treatment. In the hundred and fifteen autistic children studied, ninety-four percent had IQs that fell within the retarded range at the time of the initial evaluation. These IQs were related to the severity of the symptoms and were shown to be predictors of later school performance. From this study DeMyer concluded that those children with IQs lower than forty do not respond well to treatment and educational programs. Those with IQs higher than fifty, however, do respond to such programs; in fact, some even have a chance for borderline or "normal" function.

Summary of Follow-Up Studies and Prognostic Signs

In a recent review of all follow-up studies on autistic children, Lotter (206) reported that only five to seventeen percent of all children studied eventually achieved a "good outcome;" by "good outcome" he meant that their social life was near normal and their school or work performance was satisfactory. On the other hand, sixty-one to seventy-four percent of formerly autistic children had "very poor outcomes," which meant that they were incapable of leading any kind of independent life. Lotter concluded that although predictors of outcome were not clear and consistent, the best indicators were presence of communicative speech, IQ test performance, degree of overall severity of the disorder, and work-school ratings. He also stated that the presence of demonstrable brain dysfunction or damage is associated with more severely retarded functioning and negatively correlated with good outcome.

After considering these findings on measured intelligence of autistic individuals, we may conclude that there are different levels of functional intelligence within the syndrome of autism. The higher the level of functional intelligence, as reflected by IQ, the better the chances of approaching normal adjustment. Kanner's original notion that autistic children have "good cognitive potential" is not confirmed by the findings of these long-range studies. Although young autistic children usually show isolated fragments of ability that distinguish them from typically retarded children, most do not achieve a functional intelligence that leads to adjustment. Those few who do achieve it usually show it at an early age in their intelligence test performance.

One other early prognostic sign should be mentioned. An earlier chapter noted that the young autistic child typically refuses to play with conventional toys or uses them inappropriately. He may impatiently flip them aside or use them in activities unrelated to their purpose. If, however, he does show appropriate play with toys by age four or five, this may be regarded as a positive sign (207).

To summarize the conclusions of the long-range research reviewed in this chapter, several interrelated factors appear to be associated with later adjustment of the autistic child:

1. The use of language for communication before age five or six has been found to be a crucial sign in most studies. The child who displays some functional speech by this age stands a chance to achieve some adjustment; the child who is mute stands virtually no chance at all.

2. The measured intelligence of the young child is also a predictive sign; the higher the IQ, the closer the child will approach normal adjustment. The same rule, of course, holds for typically retarded children. While autistic children differ in many respects from most retarded children, it appears that they, too, represent different levels of functional intelligence.

3. The presence of seizures and other signs of neurological dysfunction appear to be correlated with the severity of the retardation and long-term impairment.

4. The play activity of the child serves as another prognostic sign. If he plays appropriately with toys before age five or so, the prospects for later adjustment are better.

5. The severity of the early symptoms shown by the child also seems to be associated with later adjustment; the more pronounced these symptoms, the lower the probability of response to treatment and educational programs.

6. Placement in an institution for the retarded is negatively related to later adjustment. As was pointed out earlier, this cannot be clearly indicted as a negative influence since it is probable that the most severely impaired child is referred for residential care in the first place. Nevertheless, this finding suggests that all

alternative modes of treatment for the child should be exhausted before long-term residential placement is considered.

7. Traditional psychotherapy, if not a negative factor, is certainly not a positive one for long-range outcome of autistic children. Those few adults who have "recovered" have apparently done so in spontaneous fashion, irrespective of professional treatment.

It is still too early, however, to assess the long-term influence of recently developed approaches to treatment and evaluation of autistic children. As noted in past chapters, behavior therapy has been effective in developing language, eliminating self-destructive behavior, and making the child more accessible and manageable at home and school. Comprehensive programs, such as TEACCH, that combine home treatment and structured special educational classes also have enhanced the adaptation and learning of autistic children, especially if the child begins these programs at a very early age. The evidence thus far, however, suggests that the child's response to any program is still dependent to a large degree on his level of intelligence, use of language, and the severity of his initial symptoms.

The five-year-old autistic child, then, who shows some meaningful speech, performs fairly well on IQ tests, and plays appropriately with toys has a much better chance of achieving later adjustment than an autistic child of the same age who shows no speech or only echolalia, functions poorly on IQ tests or is "untestable," and uses toys in stereotypic, meaningless fashion. The latter child will probably be the one to require intensive care for the rest of his life. The former, although having better prospects for a "good outcome," will not, however, achieve "normality" in a strict sense. Even those autistic children who demonstrate the best combination of favorable prognostic signs will probably as adolescents and adults have significant residual problems in social and cognitive functioning; these problems will include extreme shyness and introversion, literalness, deficient social judgment and empathy, and difficulty in forming intimate relationships. As pointed out earlier in this chapter, Kanner's first case, Donald, despite his relatively good adjustment as an adult, shows vestiges of autism in some of these areas.

We may wonder what these autistic persons, like Donald, who have recovered to some extent, can tell us of their childhood. As Bemporad (208) stated it, "one of the elusive yet intriguing questions that occurs to almost anyone who deals with autistic children is an overwhelming curiosity about what they are experiencing or thinking" (p. 192). Bemporad attempted to answer this question through a series of interviews with Jerry, a thirty-one-year-old man who had been diagnosed as autistic at four years of age by Kanner himself. Jerry is one of the few who has achieved a "good outcome" although he cannot be considered normal. According to Bemporad, Jerry summarized his childhood experiences as consisting of the two predominant states of confusion and terror:

> The recurrent theme that ran through all of Jerry's recollections was that of living in a frightening world presenting painful stimuli that could not be mastered. Noises were unbearably loud, smells overpowering. Nothing seemed constant; everything was unpredictable and strange. Animate beings were a particular problem. Dogs were remembered as eerie and terrifying. As a child, he believed they were somehow humanoid (since they moved of their own volition, etc.), yet they were not really human, a puzzle that mystified him. They were especially unpredictable; they could move quickly without provocation. To this day, Jerry is phobic of dogs.
>
> He was also frightened of other children, fearing that they might hurt him in some way. He could never predict or understand their behavior. Elementary school was remembered as a horrifying experience. The classroom was total confusion and he always felt he "would go to pieces." (p. 192)

Bemporad reported further that Jerry, in reconstructing his childhood, failed to mention any relationship with family members; they seemed to have little significance in his life. In adolescence, the original fear was still there but he wanted some sort of relationship with others. He had no notion, however, of how to approach other people and therefore suffered realistic rejections. Even at the time of the interview, when he was thirty-one years of age, Jerry still showed a high degree of social ineptness and poor social adjustment.

As the cases of Donald and Jerry illustrate, even the most successful autistic persons fail to achieve a full, normal life in social and personal spheres. Although they may complete high school or college and hold a regular job, they apparently never enjoy the intimate and emotionally rewarding relationships that constitute the basic fabric of life for most of us. But the outcome, according to current statistics, will be far worse for most autistic children, especially those that fail to show the early favorable signs.

However, the factors summarized above should not be viewed as final answers to the question of long-term prognosis in autistic children, nor should they be regarded as infallible predictors of success or failure. For if this occurs, we slip into the trap of making self-fulfilling prophecies. The five-year-old autistic child with no language and an IQ less than forty should not be automatically written off as hopeless and relegated to a custodial setting. The prophecy that he will never adjust will, of course, be fulfilled if we fail to give him a chance in various treatment and educational programs, if we fail to try new things with him. Instead we should view the discouraging results of these follow-up studies as a challenge to develop and test new treatment programs that may reach more effectively the child who now has the poor prognosis for adolescence and adulthood.

Epilogue

It is not up to me to decide between the various labels that are offered to describe my child's condition, but there is one that I have come to think is clearly inapplicable. My child is not, I think, a "disturbed child." Now and then things happen that are too much for her capacities, and these disturb her. But the longer I watch her, the better I know her, and the more there is to know, the more I am convinced that what we are concerned with is not a disturbance but a lack. The screw is not loose, it is missing . . . ." (114, p. 260-261)

We started by looking at the strange, unsettling symptoms of the autistic child. Symptoms that, at first glance, may have drawn us toward the conclusion that here indeed is an emotionally disturbed child, a child who displays all sorts of bizarre, crazy behavior—a child with a loose screw. We may have assumed further that these symptoms, with their conspicious emotional and social components, must surely stem from emotional and social influences in the child's early environment. Here is a beautiful, well-formed child who was potentially normal until he sensed, soon after coming into the world, that he would be hurt by hostile people; so he developed an intricate behavioral system that precluded interaction with them. With these assumptions planted firmly in our minds, we may have seen the pieces fall into place when we read the initial description of the parents as

169

aloof, emotionally frigid individuals. These individuals, we may have concluded, undoubtedly created the cold, rejecting psychological atmosphere that prompted the child to withdraw from the world.

Unfortunately, many professionals concerned with autistic children adopted this beguiling line of reasoning and clung to this conclusion despite the absence of confirming evidence. This "pernicious hypothesis," as Rimland (7) has rightfully called it, was translated to an unquestioned verity in their minds. Many parents, already confused and guilt-ridden, have served as convenient scapegoats for the underlying ignorance and scientific insecurity of the professional. They found themselves in a "damned-if-they-do, damned-if-they-don't" position. If they accepted their designated role as causal agent, they merely confirmed the foregone conclusion; if they refused to accept the role, they were omnisciently accused of using the defense mechanism of denial. In her book *The Siege* (114), Clara Park, the mother of an autistic child, wrote that the director of a clinic for autistic children in a large medical center has reported that "one of his greatest problems in treatment is the resistance parents make to the idea that they cause the disease" (p. 142).

Since the cause of autism was self-evident in the minds of many, research on the other possible causes was either pooh-poohed or viewed as heretical. Parents and children were subjected to expansive psychodynamic formulations and expensive psychotherapy which largely accomplished nothing. Fortunately, though, some parents and professionals were skeptical and refused to accept blindly the psychogenic gospel and therapeutic rites. Researchers began to regard autism as still an open issue.

This rejuvenated research, which has been considered in this book, has cast a new light not only on the possible cause of autism, but also on the basic nature of the disorder. The recent findings suggest that the parents of autistic children are really no different from most parents—maybe brighter as a whole, but certainly not the cold, intellectual stereotype found in early descriptions. There is no evidence whatsoever that they cause the disorder. In fact, the available evidence, as was noted in Chapter 9, is more consistent with the theory that the underlying cause (or causes) is organic. Further, recent experiments that have attempted to assess and define more precisely the deficits in autistic children revealed that the major defects lie more in cognitive than emotional areas, although there are certain emotional components.

The evidence suggests that the primary impairment in most autistic children is in the ability to select, perceive, and interpret incoming stimuli, including those that mediate social attachment and interaction. Autistic children have extreme difficulty in attaching meaning to these stimuli, forming concepts, and learning from experience; and most are markedly impaired in using language in a meaningful fashion. It looks, then, like many of the emotional and social symptoms, rather than being reactions to parents perceived as hostile and rejecting, are secondary reactions to this intrinsic inability to cope and make sense of the melange of subtle stimuli that convey the feelings, ideas, and ultimately the personhood of another human being. With most children, this process of discovering the personhood of other individuals comes as naturally as breathing; with autistic children, it comes with great difficulty or not at all.

Although some of the emotional and behavioral problems may recede as autistic children grow older, many of the handicaps persist even after intensive treatment. As Lovaas has stated, the autistic child can be taught eye contact with behavior modification but he does not suddenly "discover people." Traditional psychotherapy has proved to be the least effective of any approach; drug treatment has been useful in controlling some of the behavioral symptoms; and the more recently developed programs in behavior modification, structured special education, and home-based treatment have helped the children in learning certain skills and behaviors, although no cures have been effected. The response to these treatment and educational programs, of course, varies from child to child. As was emphasized in the last chapter, autistic children who stand the best chance of responding favorably to programs and making some adaptation to society are those who have IQs above fifty and show meaningful speech and appropriate play by five years of age. Rarely, however, do any autistic children achieve normal adjustment.

What, then, may we learn from the relatively short history of the study of this rare disorder?

First, we should acknowledge that with all of our scientific expertise in many areas, we still know relatively little about the complex variables that determine human behavior. All-encompassing theories that "explain" everything have not only precluded the search for causes, but have also given mental health professionals a false sense of authority which, in the case of autism, has only resulted in frustration, guilt, and expense for parents. Since their children, their money, and their happiness are involved, parents have every right to question this professional authority, especially when it is based more on theory than on fact. Professionals have the ethical responsibility, when there is a lack of empirical evidence, to appropriately qualify their speculation; or (heaven forbid!) they can admit their ignorance and simply say, "I don't know."

The history of the study and treatment of the autistic child should also make us question some of the notions about child development that are accepted as truths in professional circles and in society at large. One such belief is that most, if not all, psychological problems of childhood are induced by social experiences. This psychogenic bias, especially the hallowed tenet of maternal deprivation, has dominated our thinking for years, causing us to relegate such physical influences as genes, biochemistry, neural structure and function to insignificant roles in the development of behavior. The fact that there is a biological substrate for emotional and psychological processes has been eclipsed by the widely accepted dictum that the child's experiences are the prime shapers of how he thinks, feels, and acts; and the earlier these experiences occur, the more potent and indelible their effects on his behavior. With these ideas pervading our child-rearing beliefs and being spouted as scientific principles by authorities, many parents of autistic children held themselves responsible for their child's disorder. And if this was not enough, they were told either directly or indirectly by so-called experts that they *were* responsible. So they found themselves saddled with the guilt of having unwittingly committed some dreadful error in the early rearing of their child—an error that assumed even more terrible proportions because of its presumed irreversible effects.

But the parents' plight extended beyond the culpability assigned to them by professionals. Many professionals, in keeping with their psychogenic philosophy, advocated intensive psychotherapy for the autistic child and his parents. Many hours were wasted in trying to break through the child's emotional defenses; and many more hours wasted in trying to remedy the parental "pathology" that precipitated the child's withdrawal. The lack of therapeutic success, however, could be readily explained. There was only so much a therapist could do to change a home environment that sustains autism, and only so much he could do to correct the irreversible and omnipotent effects of maternal deprivation.

It is no wonder, then, that parents abandoned the traditional mental health approaches. The recent history of parental involvement in development of programs for special children shows that bright, concerned parents will tolerate half-baked hypotheses, professional "omniscience," and unproductive treatment programs for only so long before they begin to move on their own. This has been the case with the parents of autistic children. Through the National Society for Autistic Children, these parents have developed local educational programs and have worked for national legislation that would include autistic children in funded programs for developmentally disabled children. In the few years that they have been in existence, these special educational and treatment programs have accomplished more for the autistic child and his parents than the traditional programs have accomplished over three decades.

It is too late to undo the harm inflicted on many parents by the biases that abound in our society and too late to recover the lost time that could have been spent in productive research. Perhaps, though, the study of the autistic child will give us a new perspective on human behavior, a new appreciation for the biological capabilities of the human organism to develop into a thinking, feeling person in spite of environmental adversities, and variations in parental personalities and child-rearing techniques. Perhaps we have paid too much attention to Locke and not enough to Kant. Rather than being a blank tablet, the normal human brain at birth is an intricately wired, resilient mechanism programmed to select and categorize experience with increasing efficiency as it matures. With the autistic child, though, there appears to be a severe defect in the mechanism that interferes with its operation from the start of life or soon thereafter, and this defect has widespread and accumulating effects. To borrow the words used by Clara Park in describing her autistic daughter Elly, "the screw is not loose, it is missing."

Perhaps the most important lesson that we can learn from study of the autistic child is that the complexity of human behavior can be unraveled only through systematic, painstaking study of the behavior itself and how it relates to clearly defined external and internal variables. Theories and explanations of behavior, however profound or inviolable they may seem, should never be above our questions or experimental evaluations. Fortunately, there will always be the iconoclast in our midst who will scrutinize the explanation and say, "It ain't necessarily so." When the theories and techniques based on them are shown to be no longer useful, they should be abandoned, especially when they distort rather than clarify our observations, discourage rather than encourage research, and hurt rather than help people.

Progress has been made in understanding the disorder of autism only since researchers have focused carefully on its behavioral, social, and biological features without preconceived notions biasing observations and conclusions. Through such study we at least have been able to better define the basic deficits, gain a more objective appraisal of family characteristics, assess response to different forms of treatment and education, and determine factors related to long-term adjustment. Further research will ultimately lead to the cause (or causes) of autism, and then effective treatment and prevention may be possible. In the course of finding these causes and trying to reach the autistic child, there is no doubt that we will discover many things that we did not know about human behavior.

References

1. Kanner, L. Autistic disturbances of affective contact. *Nervous Child,* 1943, 2, 217-250. (Most of the articles by Kanner in the reference list have been reprinted in: Kanner, L. *Childhood psychosis: Initial studies and new insights.* New York: V. H. Winston & Sons, 1973.)

2. Kanner, L. Early infantile autism. *Journal of Pediatrics,* 1944, 25, 211-217.

3. Ornitz, E. M., & Ritvo, E. R. The syndrome of autism: a critical review. *American Journal of Psychiatry,* 1976, 133, 609-621.

4. Treffert, D. A. Epidemiology of infantile autism. *Archives of General Psychiatry,* 1970, 22, 431-438.

5. Lotter, V. Services for a group of autistic children in Middlesex. In J. K. Wing (Ed.), *Early childhood autism (1st ed.).* London: Pergamon Press, 1966.

6. Ritvo, E. R., & Freeman, B. J. National Society for Autistic Children definition of the syndrome of autism. *Journal of Pediatric Psychology,* 1977, 2, 146-148.

7. Rimland, B. *Infantile autism.* New York: Appleton-Century-Crofts, 1964.

8. Ornitz, E. M. Childhood autism: A review of the clinical and experimental literature. *California Medicine,* 1973, 118, 21-47.

9. Greenfeld, J. *A child called Noah.* New York: Holt, Rinehart, & Winston, 1972.

175

10. Greenfeld, J. *A place for Noah.* New York: Holt, Rinehart, & Winston, 1978.

11. Kaufman, B. N. *Son-rise.* New York: Harper & Row, 1976.

12. Vaillant, G. E. John Haslam on early infantile autism. *American Journal of Psychiatry,* 1962, *119,* 376.

13. Itard, J. M. G. *The wild boy of Aveyron.* English translation of Itard's two reports (1801, 1807) by G. Humphrey (1932), New York: Appleton-Century Crofts, 1962.

14. Wing, J. K. Kanner's syndrome: A historical introduction. In L. Wing (Ed.), *Early childhood autism (2nd ed.). Oxford: Pergamon Press, 1976.*

15. Kanner, L. The birth of early infantile autism. *Journal of Autism and Childhood Schizophrenia,* 1973, *3,* 93-95.

16. Kanner, L. Problems of nosology and psychodynamics of early infantile autism. *American Journal of Orthopsychiatry,* 1949, *19,* 416-426.

17. DSM-III: *Diagnostic and statistical manual of mental disorders (3rd edition).* New York: The American Psychiatric Association, 1980.

18. Eisenberg, L., & Kanner, L. Early infantile autism, 1943-1955. *American Journal of Orthopsychiatry,* 1956, *26,* 556-566.

19. Bakwin, H. Early infantile autism. *Journal of Pediatrics,* 1954, *45,* 492-497.

20. Clancy, H., & McBride, J. The autistic process and its treatment. *Journal of Child Psychology and Psychiatry,* 1969, *10,* 233-244.

21. Creak, M. Discussion: psychoses in childhood. *Proceedings of Royal Society of Medicine,* 1952, *45,* 797-800.

22. Rattner, L. J., & Chapman, A. H. Dangers of indiscriminate hospitalization of the preschool child. *Journal of Dentistry for Children,* 1959, *26,* 55-62.

23. Hutt, C., & Ounsted, C. The biological significance of gaze aversion with particular reference to the syndrome of infantile autism. *Behavioral Science,* 1966, *11,* 346-356.

24. Zaslow, R. W. & Breger, L. A theory and treatment of autism. In L. Breger (Ed.), *Clinical-cognitive psychology.* Englewood Cliffs, N. J.: Prentice-Hall, 1969.

25. Hefferman, A. A psychiatric study of fifty preschool children referred to hospital for suspected deafness. In G. Caplan (Ed.), *Emotional Problems of Early Childhood.* New York: Basic Books, Inc., 1955.

26. Goldfarb, W. Receptor preferences in schizophrenic children. *Archives of Neurology and Psychiatry,* 1956, *76,* 643-652.

27. Anthony, E. J. An experimental approach to the psychopathology of childhood autism. *British Journal of Medical Psychology,* 1958, *31,* 211-225.

28. Bergman, P., & Escalona, S. K. Unusual sensitivities in very young children. *Psychoanalytic Study of the Child*, 1949, *3-4*, 333-352.

29. Sherwin, A. C. Reactions to music of autistic (schizophrenic) children. *American Journal of Psychiatry*, 1953, *109*, 823-831.

30. Kanner, L. Infantile autism and the schizophrenias. *Behavioral Science*, 1965, *10*, 412-420.

31. Ritvo, S., & Provence, S. Form perception and imitation in some autistic children: Diagnostic findings and their contextual interpretation. *The Psychoanalytic Study of the Child*, 1953, 8, 155-161.

32. Kanner, L. Irrelevant and metaphorical language in early infantile autism. *American Journal of Psychiatry*, 1946, *103*, 242-245.

33. Kanner, L. The conception of wholes and parts in early infantile autism. *American Journal of Psychiatry*, 1951, *108*, 23-26.

34. Witmer, L. Orthogenic cases, XIV—Don: A curable case of arrested development due to a fear psychosis the result of shock in a three year old infant. *Psychological Clinic*, 1919-22, *13*, 97-111.

35. Berkson, G., & Davenport, R. K., Jr. Stereotyped movements of mental defectives. I. Initial survey. *American Journal of Mental Deficiency*, 1962, 66, 849-852.

36. Azrin, N. H., Kaplan, S. J., & Foxx, R. M. Autism reversal: Eliminating stereotyped self-stimulation of retarded individuals. *American Journal of Mental Deficiency*, 1973, *78*, 241-248.

37. Colbert, E., & Koegler, R. Toe walking in childhood schizophrenia. *Journal of Pediatrics*, 1958, *53*, 219-220.

38. Ornitz, E. M. & Ritvo, E. R. Perceptual inconstancy in early infantile autism. *Archives of General Psychiatry*, 1968, *18*, 76-98.

39. Sorosky, A. D., Ornitz, E. M., Brown, M. B., & Ritvo, E. R. Systematic observation of autistic behavior. *Archives of General Psychiatry*, 1968, *18*, 439-449.

40. Ornitz, E. M., Brown, M. B., & Sorosky, A. D. Environmental modification of autistic behavior. *Archives of General Psychiatry*, 1970, *22*, 560-565.

41. Ritvo, E. R., Ornitz, E. M., & LaFranchi, S. Frequency of repetitive behaviors in early infantile autism and its variants. *Archives of General Psychiatry*, 1968, *19*, 341-347.

42. Green, A. H. Self-mutilation in schizophrenic children. *Archives of General Psychiatry*, 1967, *17*, 234-244.

43. Frankel, F., & Simmons, J. Q., III. Self-injurious behavior in schizophrenic and retarded children. *American Journal of Mental Deficiency*, 1976, 5, 512-522.

44. Rothenberg, M. The rebirth of Jonny. *Harper's Magazine*, 1960, *220*, (Feb.), 57-66.

45. Churchill, D. W. *Language of autistic children*. Washington: V. H. Winston & Sons, 1978.

46. Rutter, M. (Ed.) *Infantile autism: Concepts, characteristics, and treatment*. London: Churchill Livingston, 1971.

47. Ricks, D. M., & Wing, L. Language, communication, and the use of symbols in normal and autistic children. *Journal of Autism and Childhood Schizophrenia*. 1975, *5*, 191-221.

48. Bartak, L., Rutter, M., & Cox, A. A. A comparative study of infantile autism and specific developmental receptive disorder. I. The children. *British Journal of Psychiatry*, 1975, *126*, 146-159.

49. Lord, C., & Baker, A. F. Communicating with autistic children. *Journal of Pediatric Psychology*, 1977, *2*, 181-186.

50. Hermelin, B., & O'Connor, N. *Psychological experiments with autistic children*. New York: Pergamon Press, 1970.

51. DeMyer, M. K. Motor, perceptual-motor, and intellectual disabilities of autistic children. In L. Wing (Ed.), *Early childhood autism* (2nd ed.). Oxford: Pergamon Press, 1976.

52. Ricks, D. M., & Wing, L. Language, communication, and the use of symbols. In L. Wing (Ed.), *Early childhood autism* (2nd ed.). Oxford: Pergamon Press, 1976.

53. Goldfarb, W. *Childhood schizophrenia*. Cambridge, Mass.: Harvard University Press, 1961.

54. Wing, J. K. Diagnosis, epidemiology, aetiology. In J. K. Wing (Ed.), *Early childhood autism* (1st ed.). London: Pergamon Press, 1966.

55. Morris, W. (Ed.) *The American heritage dictionary of the English language*. New York: American Heritage Dictionary, 1969.

56. Rutter, M., & Bartak, L. Causes of infantile autism: Some considerations from recent research. *Journal of Autism and Childhood Schizophrenia*, 1971, *1*, 20-32.

57. Wechsler, D. *The Wechsler intelligence scale for children—revised*. New York: The Psychological Corporation, 1974.

58. Rutter, M., & Lockyer, L. A five to fifteen year follow-up study of infantile psychosis: I. Description of the sample. *British Journal of Psychiatry*, 1967, *113*, 1169-1182.

59. Wing, L. Diagnosis, clinical description, and prognosis. In L. Wing (Ed.), *Early childhood autism* (2nd ed.). Oxford: Pergamon Press, 1976.

60. Ritvo, E. R., Ornitz, E. M., Walter, R. D., et. al. Correlation of psychiatric diagnoses and EEG findings: A double-blind study of 184 hospitalized children. *American Journal of Psychiatry*, 1970, *126*, 988-996.

61. Bender, L., & Freedman, A. M. A study of the first three years in the maturation of schizophrenic children. *Quarterly Journal of Child Behavior*, 1952, *4*, 245-272.

62. Fish, B. Involvement of the central nervous system in infants with schizophrenia. *Archives of Neurology*, 1960, *2*, 115-121.

63. Boucher, J. Articulation in early childhood autism. *Journal of Autism and Childhood Schizophrenia*, 1976, *6*, 297-302.

64. Kanner, L., & Lesser, L. I. Early infantile autism. *Pediatric Clinics of America*, 1958, *5*, 711-730.

65. Rutter, M. Behavioral and cognitive characteristics of a series of psychotic children. In J. K. Wing (Ed.), *Early childhood autism* (1st ed.). London: Pergamon Press, 1966.

66. Cobrinik, L. Unusual reading ability in severely disturbed children: clinical observation and a retrospective inquiry. *Journal of Autism and Childhood Schizophrenia*, 1974, *4*, 163-175.

67. Kanner, L. Emotional interference with intellectual functioning. *American Journal of Mental Deficiency*, 1952, *56*, 701-707.

68. Benda, C. E. Childhood schizophrenia, autism, and Heller's disease. In P. W. Bowman & H. V. Mautner (Eds.), *Mental retardation: Proceedings of the first international conference on mental retardation*. New York: Grune & Stratton, 1960.

69. O'Connell, T. S. The musical life of an autistic boy. *Journal of Autism and Childhood Schizophrenia*, 1974, *4*, 223-229.

70. Lansing, C. Letter to the Editor. *Journal of Autism and Childhood Schizophrenia*, 1975, *5*, 187-188.

71. Rutter, M., Bartak, L., & Newman, S. Autism—a central disorder of cognition and language? In M. Rutter (Ed.), *Infantile autism: Concepts, characteristics, and treatment*. London: Churchill, 1971.

72. Bartak, L., & Rutter, M. Differences between mentally retarded and normally intelligent autistic children. *Journal of Autism and Childhood Schizophrenia*, 1976, *6*, 109-120.

73. Rutter, M. Autistic children—infancy to adulthood. *Seminars in Psychiatry*, 1970, *2*, 435-450.

74. Tinbergen, N. Ethology and stress diseases. *Science*, 1974, *185*, 20-27.

75. Rimland, B. The differentiation of childhood psychoses: An analysis of checklists for 2,218 psychotic children. *Journal of Autism and Childhood Schizophrenia*, 1971, *2*, 161-174.

76. Kanner, L. The children haven't read those books. *Acta Paedopsychiatrica*, 1969, *36*, 2-11.

77. Freeman, B. J. The syndrome of autism: The problem of diagnosis in research. *Journal of Pediatric Psychology,* 1977, *2,* 142-145.

78. Freeman, B. J., & Ritvo, E. R. Diagnostic and evaluation systems: Helping the advocate cope with the "state of the art." In J. Budde (Ed.), *Advocacy and autism.* Lawrence, Kansas: University of Kansas Press, 1977.

79. Freeman, B. J. Behavioral correlates of the syndromes of autism. Paper presented at the meeting of the American Psychological Association, San Francisco, California, 1977.

80. Grossman, H. J. (Ed.). *Manual on terminology and classification in mental retardation.* Washington: American Association on Mental Deficiency, 1977.

81. Wing, L. A study of language impairments in severely retarded children. In N. O'Connor (Ed.), *Language, cognitive deficits, and retardation.* London: Butterworths, 1975.

82. Berkson, G. Abnormal stereotyped motor acts. In J. Zubin & H. F. Hunt (Eds.), *Comparative psychopathology: animal and human.* New York: Grune & Stratton, 1967.

83. Rutter, M. The development of infantile autism. *Psychological Medicine,* 1974, *4,* 147-163.

84. Rutter, M. Childhood schizophrenia reconsidered. *Journal of Autism and Childhood Schizophrenia,* 1972, *2,* 315-337.

85. Bender, L. A longitudinal study of schizophrenic children with autism. *Hospital Community Psychiatry,* 1969, *20,* 230-237.

86. Brown, J. L., & Reiser, D. E. Follow-up study of preschool children of atypical development (infantile psychosis)—later personality patterns in adaptation to maturational stress. *American Journal of Orthopsychiatry,* 1963, *33,* 336-338.

87. Darr, G. C., & Worden, F. G. Case report twenty-eight years after an infantile autistic disorder. *American Journal of Orthopsychiatry,* 1951, *21,* 559-570.

88. Bender, L. The life course of children with autism and mental retardation. In F. J. Menolascino (Ed.), *Psychiatric approaches to mental retardation.* New York: Basic Books, 1970.

89. Mahler, M. S. On child psychosis and schizophrenia: Autistic and symbiotic infantile psychosis. *Psychoanalytic Study of the Child,* 1952, *7,* 286-305.

90. Mahler, M. S. On human symbiosis and the vicissitudes of individuation. Vol. I. *Infantile Psychosis.* New York: International Universities Press, 1968.

91. Knopf, I. J. *Childhood psychopathology: A developmental approach.* Englewood Cliffs, N. J.: Prentice-Hall, 1979.

92. Wing, L. The handicaps of autistic children—a comparative study. *Journal of Child Psychology and Psychiatry*, 1969, *10*, 1-40.

93. de Hirsch, K. Differential diagnosis between aphasic and schizophrenic language in children. *Journal of Speech and Hearing Disorders*, 1967, *32*, 3-10.

94. Griffith, R., & Ritvo, E. Echolalia: Concerning the dynamics of the syndrome. *Journal of the American Academy of Child Psychiatry*, 1967, *6*, 184-193.

95. Keeler, W. R. Autistic patterns and defective communication in blind children with retrolental fibroplasia. In P. H. Hoch & J. Zubin (Eds.), *Psychopathology in communication*. New York: Grune & Stratton, 1958.

96. Chess, S. Autism in children with cogenital rubella. *Journal of Autism and Childhood Schizophrenia*, 1971, *1*, 33-47.

97. Reed, G. R. Elective mutism in children: A reappraisal. *Journal of Child Psychology and Psychiatry*, 1963, *4*, 99-107.

98. Spitz, R. A. Anaclitic depression—an inquiry into the genesis of psychiatric conditions in early childhood—I. *Psychoanalytic Study of the Child*, 1946, *2*, 313-342.

99. Durant, W. *The story of philosophy*. New York: Simon & Schuster, 1953.

100. Robinson, N. M., & Robinson, H. B. *The mentally retarded child: A psychological approach* (2nd ed.). New York: McGraw-Hill, 1976.

101. Morgan, S. B., & Jordan, R. J. Mental retardation and learning disorders. In J. G. Hughes (Ed.), *Synopsis of pediatrics, 4th Edition*. St. Louis: C. V. Mosby, 1975.

102. Clements, S. D. *Minimal brain dysfunction in children—terminology and identification*. Washington, D.C.: U. S. Department of Health, Education, & Welfare, 1966.

103. Coleman, J. C. *Abnormal psychology and modern life* (5th ed.). Glenview, Illinois: Scott, Foresman, & Co., 1976.

104. Bettleheim, B. *The empty fortress: infantile autism and the birth of self*. New York: Free Press, 1967.

105. Rutter, M. *Maternal deprivation reassessed*. Harmondsworth: Penguin, 1972.

106. Kanner, L. To what extent is early infantile autism determined by constitutional inadequacies? *Proceedings of the Association for Research in Nervous and Mental Diseases*, 1954, *33*, 378-385.

107. *Time*, July 25, 1960, p. 78.

108. Eisenberg, L. The fathers of autistic children. *American Journal of Orthopsychiatry*, 1957, *27*, 715-724.

109. Keeler, W. R. In discussion. *Psychiatric Reports of American Psychiatric*

Association, 1957, No. 7, 66-88. (Rimland, B. *Infantile autism.* New York: Appleton-Century-Crofts, 1964.)

110. Schopler, E., Andrews, C. E., & Strupp, K. Do autistic children come from upper-middle-class parents? *Journal of Autism and Developmental Disorders*, 1979, 9, 139-151.

111. McAdoo, W. G., & DeMyer, M. K. Research related to family factors in autism. *Journal of Pediatric Psychology*, 1977, 2, 162-166.

112. Wing, L. Epidemiology and theories of aetiology. In L. Wing (Ed.), *Early childhood autism* (2nd ed.). Oxford: Pergamon Press, 1976.

113. May, J. M. *A physician looks at psychiatry.* New York: John Day, 1958.

114. Park, C. *The siege.* Boston: Little, Brown and Company, 1967.

115. Hall, M. H. A conversation with Bruno Bettelheim. *Psychology Today*, 1969, 2, 21-23.

116. Eberhardy, F. The view from the couch. *Journal of Child Psychology and Psychiatry*, 1967, 8, 257-263.

117. Tinbergen, N. *Social behavior in animals, with specific reference to vertebrates.* New York: Wiley, 1965.

118. Tinbergen, N. *The animal in its world: Exploration of an ethologist, 1932-1972.* London: Allen & Unwin, 1972.

119. Ferster, C. B. Positive reinforcement and behavioral deficits of autistic children. *Child Development*, 1961, *32*, 437-456.

120. Ferster, C. B. The autistic child. *Psychology Today*, 1968, *2*, 35-37; 61.

121. O'Gorman, G. *The nature of childhood autism.* London: Butterworths, 1970.

122. Lorenz, K. Companionship in bird life. In C. Schiller (Ed.), *Instinctive behavior.* New York: International Universities Press, 1957.

123. Bowlby, J. *Attachment and loss (Vol. 1, Attachment).* New York: Basic Books, 1969.

124. Kanner, L. *Childhood psychosis: Initial studies and new insights.* New York: V. H. Winston & Sons, 1973.

125. Rimland, B. Freud is dead: New directions in the treatment of mentally ill children. *Distinguished Lectures in Special Education*, University of Southern California, June 1970, 33-48.

126. Fantz, R. L. The origins of form perception. *Scientific American*, 1961, *204*, 66-72.

127. Gibson, E. J., & Walk, R. D. The "visual cliff." *Scientific American*, 1960, *202*, 64-71.

128. McCall, R. B., & Melson, W. H. Complexity, contour, and area as determinants of attention in infants. *Developmental Psychology*, 1970, *3*, 343-349.

129. Bower, T. G. R. The visual world of infants. *Scientific American,* 1966, *215,* 80-92.

130. Bower, T. G. R. *Development in infancy.* San Francisco: W. H. Freeman, 1974.

131. Flavell, J. H. *The developmental psychology of Jean Piaget.* New York: Van Nostrand, 1963.

132. Bruner, J. S. The course of cognitive growth. *American Psychologist,* 1964, *19,* 1-15.

133. Bruner, J. S. On cognitive growth, I and II. In J. S. Bruner, R. R. Olver, & P. M. Greenfield (Eds.), *Studies in cognitive growth.* New York: Wiley, 1966.

134. Sheridan, M. D. The child's acquisition of codes of personal and interpersonal communication. In M. Rutter & J. A. M. Martin (Eds.), *The child with delayed speech.* Clinics in Developmental Medicine, No. 43. London: Heinemann, 1972.

135. Thomas, L. *The lives of a cell.* New York: Viking Press, 1974.

136. Chomsky, N. *Language and mind.* New York: Harcourt, Brace, & World, 1968.

137. Rutter, M. Concepts of autism: A review of research. *Journal of Child Psychology and Psychiatry,* 1968, *9,* 1-25.

138. Ornitz, E. M. The modulation of sensory input and motor output in autistic children. In E. Schopler & R. J. Reichler (Eds.), *Psychopathology and child development.* New York: Plenum Press, 1976.

139. Hutt, C. & Hutt, S. J. *Direct observations and the measurement of behavior.* Springfield, Illinois: Charles C. Thomas, 1970.

140. Hutt, S. J., & Hutt, C. (Eds.). *Behavior studies in psychiatry.* New York: Pergamon Press, 1970.

141. Hutt, C., Hutt, S., Lee, D., & Ounsted, C. A behavioral and electroencephalographic study of autistic children. *Journal of Psychiatric Research,* 1965, *3,* 181-197.

142. DesLauriers, A. M., & Carlson, C. F. *Your child is asleep.* Homewood, Illinois: The Dorsey Press, 1969.

143. Routtenberg, A. The two arousal hypothesis: Reticular formation and limbic system. *Psychological Review,* 1968, *75,* 51-80.

144. Martin, H. P., & Rodeheffer, M. A. The psychological impact of abuse on children. *Journal of Pediatric Psychology,* 1976, *1,* 12-16.

145. Muir, M. F. Psychological and behavioral characteristics of abused children. *Journal of Pediatric Psychology,* 1976, *1,* 16-19.

146. Creak, M., & Ini, S. Families of psychotic children. *Journal of Child Psychology and Psychiatry,* 1960, *1,* 156-175.

147. Morgan, S. B. Development and distribution of intellectual and

adaptive skills in Down Syndrome children. *Mental Retardation*, 1979, *17*, 247-249.

148. Farmer, T. W. (Ed.). *Pediatric neurology* (2nd ed.). New York: Harper & Row, 1975.

149. Bigelow, N., Roizin, L., & Kaufman, M. A. Psychoses with Huntington's Chorea. In S. Arieti (Ed.), *American Handbook of Psychiatry* (Vol. 2). New York: Basic Books, 1959.

150. Spence, M. A. Genetic studies. In E. R. Ritvo (Ed.), *Autism: Diagnosis, current research and management.* New York: Halstead/Wiley, 1976.

151. Folstein, S., & Rutter, M. Infantile autism: A genetic study of 21 twin pairs. *Journal of Child Psychology and Psychiatry*, 1977, *18*, 297-321.

152. Creak, E. M. Childhood psychosis. A review of 100 cases. *British Journal of Psychiatry*, 1963, *109*, 84-89.

153. Cohen, D. J. Testimony before U. S. House of Representatives. *National Society for Autistic Children Newsletter*, June 1974, 6, 10.

154. Molinary, S. V. & Morgan, S. B. An evaluation of the PKU screening and treatment program at the University of Tennessee Child Development Center. Paper presented at the Neuroscience Fall Festival, Memphis, 1974.

155. Chess, S. Follow-up report on autism in congenital rubella. *Journal of Autism and Childhood Schizophrenia*, 1977, *7*, 69-81.

156. Robinson, H. B., & Robinson, N. M. *The mentally retarded child: A psychological approach* (1st ed.). New York: McGraw-Hill, 1965.

157. Ford, F. R. *Diseases of the nervous system* (6th ed.). Springfield, Illinois: Charles Thomas, 1973.

158. Rank, B. Intensive study and treatment of pre-school children who show marked personality deviations or "atypical development," and their parents. In G. Caplan (Ed.), *Emotional Problems of Early Childhood.* New York: Basic Books, 1955.

159. Piggott, L. R. Overview of selected basic research in autism. *Journal of Autism and Developmental Disorders*, 1979, *9*, 199-218.

160. Hauser, S., DeLong, G., & Rosman, N. Pneumographic findings in the infantile autism syndrome: A correlation with temporal lobe disease. *Brain*, 1975, *98*, 667-668.

161. Darby, J. K. Neuropathologic aspects of psychosis in children. *Journal of Autism and Childhood Schizophrenia*, 1976, *6*, 339-352.

162. Goldfarb, W. *Growth and change of schizophrenic children: A longitudinal study.* New York: Wiley, 1974.

163. Rutter, M., & Bartak, L. Special education treatment of autistic children: A comparative study. II: Follow-up findings and implications for services. *Journal of Child Psychology and Psychiatry*, 1973, *14*, 241-270.

164. Chance, P. A conversation with Ivar Lovaas. *Psychology Today*, 1974, 7, 76-84.

165. Rimland, B. Operant conditioning: Breakthrough in the treatment of mentally ill children. In E. P. Trapp & P. Himelstein (Eds.), *Readings on the exceptional child* (2nd ed.). New York: Appleton-Century-Crofts, 1972.

166. Bettelheim, B. Joey: A "mechanical boy." *Scientific American*, 1959, 200, 116-217.

167. Roiphe, H. Childhood psychosis, self and object. *The Psychoanalytic Study of the Child*, 1973, 28, 131-145.

168. Lorenz, K. *King Solomon's ring*. New York: Crowell, 1952.

169. Blauvelt, H. Dynamics of the mother-newborn relationship in goats. In B. Schaffner (Ed.), *Group Processes*. New York: Macy Foundation, 1955.

170. Scott, J. P. *Animal behavior*. Chicago: University of Chicago Press, 1958.

171. Huxley, A. L. *Brave new world*. New York: Harper & Row, 1946.

172. Condon, R. *The Manchurian candidate*. New York: McGraw-Hill, 1959.

173. Wilson, J. A. Burgess *A clockwork orange*. New York: W. W. Norton, 1963.

174. Ferster, C. B., & DeMyer, M. A method for the experimental analysis of the behavior of autistic children. *American Journal of Orthopsychiatry*, 1962, 32, 89-98.

175. Wolf, M. M., Risely, T., & Mees, H. Application of operant conditioning procedures to the behavior problems of an autistic child. *Behaviour Research and Therapy*, 1964, 1, 305-312.

176. Wolf, M. M., Risely, T., Johnson, M., Harris, F., & Allen, E. Application of operant conditioning procedures to the behavior problems of an autistic child: A follow-up and extension. *Behaviour Research and Therapy*, 1967, 5, 103-111.

177. Hewett, F. M. Teaching speech to an autistic child through operant conditioning. *American Journal of Orthopsychiatry*, 1965, 35, 927-936.

178. Bandura, A. *Principles of behavior modification*. New York: Holt, Rinehart, & Winston, 1969.

179. Metz, J. R. Conditioning generalized imitation in autistic children. *Journal of Experimental Child Psychology*, 1965, 2, 389-399.

180. Lovaas, O. I., Berberich, J. P., Perloff, B. F., & Schaeffer, B. Acquisition of imitative speech by schizophrenic children. *Science*, 1966. 151, 705-707.

181. Lovaas, O. I., & Schreibman, L. Stimulus overselectivity of autistic children in a two-stimulus situation. *Behaviour Research and Therapy*, 1971, 2, 305-310.

182. Lovaas, O. I. *The autistic child: Language development through behavior modification.* New York: Irvington Publishers, Inc., 1977.

183. Lovaas, O. I., Koegel, R., Simmons, J. Q., & Long, J. S. Some generalization and follow-up measures on autistic children in behavior therapy. *Journal of Applied Behavior Analysis,* 1973, 6, 131-165.

184. Lovaas, O. I., Freitas, L., Nelson, K., & Whalen, C. The establishment of imitation and its use for the development of complex behavior in schizophrenic children. *Behaviour Research and Therapy,* 1967, 5, 171-181.

185. Lovaas, O. I., Schreibman, L., & Koegel, R. L. A behavior modification approach to the treatment of autistic children. In E. Schopler & R. J. Reichler (Eds.), *Psychopathology and child development.* New York: Plenum Press, 1976.

186. Lovaas, O. I., & Simmons, J. Q. Manipulation of self-destruction in three retarded children. *Journal of Applied Behavior Analysis,* 1969, 2, 143-157.

187. Tate, B. G., & Baroff, G. S. Aversive control of self-injurious behavior in a psychotic boy. *Behaviour Research and Therapy,* 1966, 4, 281-287.

188. Bucher, B. & King, L. Generalization of punishment effects in the deviant behavior of a psychotic child. *Behavior Therapy,* 1971, 2, 68-77.

189. Risely, T. The effects and side effects of punishing autistic behaviors of a deviant child. *Journal of Applied Behavior Analysis,* 1968, 1, 21-34.

190. Lichstein, K. L., & Schreibman, L. Employing electric shock with autistic children: A review of the side effects. *Journal of Autism and Childhood Schizophrenia,* 1976, 6, 163-173.

191. Baumeister, Alan A., & Baumeister, Alfred A. Suppression of repetitive self-injurious behavior by contingent inhalation of aromatic ammonia. *Journal of Autism and Childhood Schizophrenia,* 1978, 8, 71-77.

192. Skinner, B. F. *Beyond freedom and dignity.* New York: Alfred A. Knopf, 1972.

193. Rimland, B. A risk/benefit perspective on the use of aversives. *Journal of Autism and Childhood Schizophrenia,* 1978, 8, 100-104.

194. National Society for Autistic Children. NSAC white paper on behavior modification with autistic children. *NSAC Newsletter,* August, 1975, 7, 14-15.

195. Schopler, E. Toward reducing behavior problems in autistic children. *Journal of Autism and Childhood Schizophrenia,* 1976, 6, 1-13.

196. Reichler, R. J., & Schopler, E. Developmental therapy: A program model for providing individualized services in the community. In E. Schopler & R. J. Reichler (Eds.), *Psychopathology and Child Development.* New York: Plenum Press, 1976.

197. Reichler, R. J., & Schopler, E. Observations on the nature of human relatedness. *Journal of Autism and Childhood Schizophrenia*, 1971, *1*, 283-296.

198. Sloan, J. L., & Schopler, E. Some thoughts about developing programs for autistic adolescents. *Journal of Pediatric Psychology*, 1977, *2*, 187-190.

199. Campbell, M., Geller, B., & Cohen, I. L. Current status of drug research and treatment with autistic children. *Journal of Pediatric Psychology*, 1977, *2*, 153-161.

200. Rimland, B., Callaway, E., & Dreyfus, P. The effect of high doses of Vitamin B6 on autistic children: A double-blind crossover study. *American Journal of Psychiatry*, 1978, *4*, 472-475.

201. Kanner, L. Follow-up study of eleven autistic children originally reported in 1943. *Journal of Autism and Childhood Schizophrenia*, 1971, *1*, 119-145.

202. Kanner, L., Rodriguez, A., & Ashenden, B. How far can autistic children go in matters of social adaptation? *Journal of Autism and Childhood Schizophrenia*, 1972, *2*, 9-33.

203. Rutter, M., Greenfeld, D., & Lockyer, L. A five to fifteen year follow-up study of infantile psychosis: II. Social and behavioral outcome. *British Journal of Psychiatry*, 1967, *113*, 1183-1199.

204. DeMyer, M. K., Barton, S., DeMyer, W. E., Norton, J. A., Allen, J., & Steele, R. Prognosis in autism: A follow-up study. *Journal of Autism and Childhood Schizophrenia*, 1973, *3*, 199-246.

205. DeMyer, M. K., Barton, S., Alpern, G. D., Kimberlin, C., Allen, J., Yang, E., & Steele, R. The measured intelligence of autistic children. *Journal of Autism and Childhood Schizophrenia*, 1974, *4*, 42-60.

206. Lotter, V. Follow-up studies. In M. Rutter & E. Schopler (Eds.), *Autism: A reappraisal of concepts and treatment.* New York: Plenum Press, 1978.

207. Brown, J. Prognosis from presenting symptoms of preschool children with atypical development. *American Journal of Orthopsychiatry*, 1960, *30*, 382-390.

208. Bemporad, Jules, R. Adult recollection of a formerly autistic child. *Journal of Autism and Developmental Disorders*, 1979, *9*, 179-197.

Name Index

188

Subject Index

191